Advance Praise

Over the years I have followed Pam Leo's laudable work as a teacher of parents and expecting parents. No other issue facing us today is so critical as this work of hers, re-establishing parental bonding with infant-child as nature intended. Indeed, our survival as a nation and species is dependent on this reconnection. And here is a concise, simple, eminently readable and instructive summary of the knowledge Pam has gained through these years of devoted service. I can't recommend this book highly enough and will surely promote it at every opportunity.

Joseph Chilton Pearce, author, *Magical Child*

Connection Parenting is utterly transformational. If all new (and seasoned) parents and grandparents read and applied its wisdom, the world would be transformed. Bravo!

Christiane Northrup, MD, author, *Mother-Daughter Wisdom* (Bantam, 2005), *The Wisdom of Menopause* (Bantam, 2001), and *Women's Bodies, Women's Wisdom* (Bantam, 1998)

Connection Parenting is the book we will all wish our parents had read when we were born and passed on to us when our children were born. For parents and grandparents who want the best for their children of any age, *Connection Parenting* contains the sacred grandmother wisdom that will reconnect us with our children.

Suzanne Arms, Founder of Birthing The Future, author, *Immaculate Deception*

Our best hope for transforming the lives of children is connection parenting.

John W. Travis, MD, MPH, author, *Wellness Workbook*, cofounder Alliance for Transforming the Lives of Children

Advance Praise

Connection Parenting heralds the encouraging news that parenting really is evolving, and with it, humanity. Pam Leo gently, irresistibly, invites us to cross over from the habitual and unconscious coercion of our children, to conscious connection with them. Empowering, simple, and undeniably true, *Connection Parenting* will help to change the face of parenting, as we know it."   Kali Wendorf, editor *byronchild* magazine - Australia

Connection Parenting speaks to the very heart of what both children and parents need in order to thrive, rather than merely survive...connection. Supporting parents in strengthening the parent-child bond is the responsibility of each and every one of us, and the prerequisite to the well-being of our world.

> Meryn Callander, President and cofounder *Alliance for Transforming the Lives of Children* (aTLC)

Every child, every parent needs Connection Parenting. Pam Leo's brilliant work, *Connection Parenting*, is on the top of our reading list.

> Ray Castellino, DC., RCST Clinic Director: BEBA, Director: Castellino Prenatal and Birth Training, Adjunct Faculty: Santa Barbara Graduate Institute

As a mother and a grandmother, reading *Connection Parenting* filled me with both great sadness and great joy. That I didn't have the book's crucial information when I was raising my children makes me sad. My joy is that I will give Pam Leo's book to my sons and daughter. With its wonderful information, I know that my grandchildren will be able to rejoice in their enriched childhood. This book gives adults tools to rewrite and repair our old tapes so that we can better communicate with our children and with one another.

> Marilyn Milos, RN, Founder and Executive Director National Organization of Circumcision Information Resource Centers (NOCIRC)

Connection parenting is the perfect extension of in-arms, continuum, or attachment parenting with our little ones—and it fits in our present day culture in a way that makes it accessible to families from all kinds of backgrounds and belief systems.

Barbara Wishingrad, Founder and President,
The Rebozo Way Project

Pam Leo's Connection Parenting urges us to use what time we DO have to connect with our children, and to make an effort to create that special one-on-one time. Her poignant words offer a positive and proactive approach to parenting within today's limitations and pressures, without a load of guilt and blame placed on busy parents.

Jen Noble, Editor/Publisher *Parent & Family*

Among the hundreds of parenting books available today, Pam Leo's handbook, **Connection Parenting**, is like a breath of fresh air. Don't be deceived by its simplicity. She has captured the essence of good parenting with profound and compassionate advice.

Aletha Solter, Ph.D., Director of the Aware Parenting Institute,
author, *The Aware Baby*

Pam Leo dares to step outside the box to teach parents what it takes to truly connect with a child. Her "minimum daily requirements" of connection are the vitamins of everyday parenting.

Bonnie Harris, author, *When Your Kids Push Your Buttons and What You Can Do About It*

I am delighted with Pam Leo's book. It has a host of practical ideas anyone of us can use to enjoy our children or grandchildren.

Diane Gossen, author, *It's All About WE; Rethinking Discipline Using Restitution*

Advance Praise

I loved **Connection Parenting** because it gently encouraged me to connect with my kids in ways I hadn't quite heard before. Thanks Pam, for sharing this wisdom in a powerful yet uncomplicated way.
Tom Adams, Founder, KidFlourish

Pam Leo's **Connection Parenting** is a breath of fresh air. It is sure to sweep away cobwebs of confusion parents typically discover when looking for answers in the burgeoning landscape of parenting books and their often conflicting philosophies.

Grounded in field-tested experience for three decades, Pam's illuminating insights into the components of creating and preserving the sacred bond between parent and child picks up where basic attachment parenting and Continuum Concept recommendations end. This readable book offers practical, compassionate parenting tools that are sure to make it an instant classic. This is the parenting book I have been waiting for! Thank you Pam!
Lisa Reagan, co-founder Families for Natural Living
US Contributing Editor, *byronchild* magazine
Parent Representative, Holistic Pediatric Association

The only solution to the unsustainable skyrocketing cost of medical care is prevention. The groundbreaking book **Connection Parenting** powerfully and effectively addresses root causes of many ills in our society—alienation, violence, substance abuse, depression and other mental illnesses. Pam Leo's clear vision of how to foster bonding and attachment at the beginning of life and to sustain it through continuing connection with children offers practical assistance for families everywhere. Connection parenting offers true hope for preventing the unsustainable skyrocketing cost of medical care in our society today.
Kent W. Peterson, MD, FACPM, FACOEM, former Executive Vice President American College of Preventive Medicine

As a family physician I advised a lot of parents on issues around child raising. I took Pam's course, and have recommended it to countless patients over the years. The feedback was consistently positive. It's great she's making this information more accessible, I love idea of book/parenting groups coming together to learn and practice connection parenting. This book will have an Oprah sticker on it before you know it!

Leigh D.Baker, D.O.

Pam Leo's **Connection Parenting** work has transformed our family interactions and continues to bring forth the best in all of us. Her work in its purest form creates a paradigm shift so profound that it not only alters one's perspective of children and childhood, but also gives us an opportunity to view the adults around us with deeper compassion and less judgment. Leo has attained the level of Mastery of the Interpersonal Dynamic, giving a new generation of human beings hope for having a childhood from which they need not recover.

Anne Archambault, CH, parent

The parents of the children in my Brain Gym practice and the students in my courses are very eager to learn from all Pam's years of experience and from her deep understanding and profound honoring of the uniqueness of each individual child. I'll just keep a supply of her books in my office—the parents' "Bible" and encourage each family to buy a copy. **Connection Parenting** is the perfect baby present for every new parent.

Beth Stoddard, MBA, Licensed Edu-K Consultant
and Brain Gym® Instructor

Advance Praise

Pam Leo taught her Connection Parenting series, "Meeting the Needs of Children" several times at our halfway house for women in early recovery from alcohol and drug addiction. Some of the participants were women trying to regain custody of their children, some had grown children, and others were hoping to have a family in the future. Without exception, the women found that by learning about Connection Parenting they changed they way they saw their children, their parents, their families.

Pam's gentle and compassionate exploration of the human developmental need for connection allowed many women here [in our program] to greatly appreciate their own need for connection, as children, as adults, in addiction, and in recovery. She gave them a unique, non-judgmental language for understanding human relationships based on the natural and vital bonds between us all.

Teresa Valliere, LCSW, CCS
Crossroads For Women, Inc.

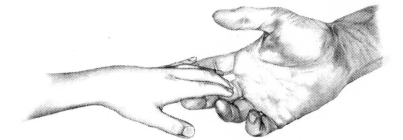

Connection Parenting:

Parenting through Connection instead of Coercion, through Love instead of Fear

By Pam Leo

Wyatt-MacKenzie Publishing, Inc.
DEADWOOD, OREGON

Dedication

To the children of the world,
this is a gift of love from me, and all the children
who told me what to say.

Pam Leo

Connection Parenting: Parenting through Connection
instead of Coercion, through Love instead of Fear

SECOND EDITION

Wyatt-MacKenzie Publishing, Inc., Deadwood, OR
www.WyMacPublishing.com (541) 964-3314
Requests for permission or further information should be addressed to:
Wyatt-MacKenzie Publishing, 15115 Highway 36, Deadwood, Oregon 97430

Cover illustration by Kelley Cunningham, www.kelleysart.com
Index by Pueblo Indexing & Publishing Services, www.puebloindexing.com

Printed in the United States of America

Connection Parenting Disclaimer:
Connection Parenting addresses the challenging behaviors caused by unmet
emotional needs, specifically the need for human connection.

Lack of adequate connection is not the cause of all challenging behaviors, nor is
more connection the cure for all challenging behaviors.

Many children are diagnosed with learning problems and behavior disorders caused
by physical and/or emotional sensitivities. Connection Parenting can reduce the
amount and intensity of these children's challenging behaviors by not compounding
their sensitivity with unmet- emotional-need behaviors. However, children with
sensitivity caused behaviors and their parents will need other support to address
those challenging behaviors in the various environments in which they occur.

Foreword

As the executive director of the Holistic Pediatric Association (HPA) and a mother seeking to be the best parent I can be, I am delighted that Pam Leo has written *Connection Parenting*. At last, we have a parenting book that gets to the heart of what it takes for children to truly thrive and be happy and healthy.

Many parents will wish this book had been around from the beginning of their parenting experience, but this well-written, practical guide makes it clear that we can begin right now. As Pam points out, "parents are always doing the best they can with the information, resources, and support they have at any given moment. It is never too late to create a stronger connection with our children." We can toss out the useless guilt about what we didn't know, or have access to, when they were younger, and begin, right now, to turn around our relationships with our children.

The more connected and in tune parents are with their children, the more they can trust their own wisdom in knowing how to treat them. The HPA promotes discarding the notion of pediatricians in an authoritarian role, and replacing it with a new paradigm of partnership between parents and pediatricians working in the best interest of the child. Parents are the "experts" when it comes to their own children and already have the innate wisdom to know what to do. However, we must deeply connect and bond with our children, and with our own inner guidance, to sense what is going on with them. Otherwise we get caught up in our omnipresent fear of disease, of going against established protocols, and of being judged. This fear may lead us to follow the "norm" and prevent us from making choices that are best for our children.

In our pediatric seminars for practitioners, HPA teachers talk about paying attention to the family dynamics and what's going on with the child in relationship to the family. Children need to feel valued, listened to, and honored. Addressing the emotional stress of the child is at the heart of holistic pediatrics. How many chronic diseases might begin to disappear once parents begin to deeply connect with their children and become more in tune with their children's emotional needs?

There is a strong psycho-emotional correlation to illness. Disconnection and lack of a strong parent-child bond can be the underlying cause of many illnesses. When parents become aware of what may be happening emotionally, and begin to meet the emotional needs of the child, the symptoms of many chronic illnesses may subside.

Our most important job as parents is to create and maintain a strong bond and loving connection with our children. This is the key to our children's happiness and optimal health and development. *Connection Parenting* tells us how to do this in a helpful, clear, and encouraging way. It shows us how to meet children's emotional needs now, so they can grow up to be healthy, truly thriving, self-empowered adults.

Discipline can be a very confusing issue to parents. *Connection Parenting* delves into the true meaning of discipline and offers new skills and tools for true discipline through connection. Pam Leo describes how to listen to and talk to our children so that they feel loved and heard, and explains the difference between punishment and discipline. Pam says; "The goal of true parental discipline is not to control children's behavior by hurting them when their behavior is unacceptable, but rather to teach children to do what is right. We cannot control anyone's behavior but our own. We can learn to decode children's behavior and respond to their needs, instead of react to their behaviors."

Connection Parenting is a compassionate, insightful, and timely gift to parents. Pam Leo celebrates the true essence of children, shines the light on children's emotional needs, and explains why children's unmet needs are the cause of most behavior problems.

I have read no other parenting book with as much potential and impetus for change in this wounded society where many individuals' needs were not met as children. *Connection Parenting* provides the tools to help us to heal hurt and disconnection and create the connection children need to be their optimal selves.

Happy, well-connected children who feel valued are healthier and more whole on all levels. When we follow the guidance given in this book, we will have a strong, positive influence in our children's lives. In addition, we will help them to develop a connection with their own true essence and happiness so that they can become the unlimited individuals they have the potential to be. When we connect with our children on a regular basis, we teach them to connect with themselves, and this is the greatest gift we can give to anyone.

I sincerely encourage parents to follow the wisdom put forth here and make it a priority to create a strong, loving bond with your children. By following the guidance in this book, we can begin to turn the tide, and create a different world in which people love, honor, and respect themselves and each other, a world of true health, harmony, and peace.

~ Jane Sheppard
Executive Director
Holistic Pediatric Association
Santa Rosa, CA

Table of Contents

We are always parenting the best we can. Whether we consciously parent the opposite from our parents or we unconsciously parent the same way our parents did, our parenting is influenced by the way we were parented. We can consciously decide to keep the best and change the rest.

Respect is the foundation of connection. We teach children respect by modeling respect. We model respect by treating children with the same respect we expect.

When we learn how children heal their emotional hurts, we gain a new level of confidence and skill in responding to crying, anger, and temper tantrums.

How we treat the child, the child will treat the world. We teach children what to believe about themselves through how we treat them. Filling their love cup builds their self-esteem and self-worth and creates connection.

Connecting through Communication that Builds Relationship
Whether communication leads to connection and cooperation or disconnection and conflict depends on how we communicate.

Connecting through Decoding Children's Behavior
Children communicate their emotional hurts and needs through their behavior. When we learn to recognize children's acting-out behavior as a communication of an unmet need, we can respond to children's needs instead of react to their behavior.

Connecting with Our Own Needs
Parents have needs too. Families work best when everyone's needs are met.

Preface

Dear Reader,

I once read, "People don't care how much you know until they know how much you care." When I became a parent more than thirty years ago, I wanted to learn how to nurture children so my two daughters could grow up to have the best life possible. The information in this book is the result of my search for answers.

I have independently studied child development, psychology, sociology, and anthropology for more than thirty years. Every new book I read contained another piece of the parenting puzzle. For twenty-two years, I provided family childcare for children, ages two through ten. I have more than 55,000 hours of experience being with and observing children, in addition to parenting my two daughters and co-parenting my grand-daughter. This work is a synthesis of my experience and my research.

In 1989, I created the Connection Parenting workshop series, "Meeting the Needs of Children." In sixteen years of teaching the series, I have learned as much from the parents, grand-parents, childcare providers, and teachers as I have taught. The concepts presented here have been thoroughly field-tested.

For many years parents in my classes have been asking, "When are you going to write a book about this kind of parenting?" I have wanted to write this book ever since I created the class, but I wasn't ready. I knew there were more pieces to the puzzle. I have finally accepted that I will never have **all** the pieces. So I am sharing the pieces I have.

This **Connection Parenting** book is designed to give you the experience of the Connection Parenting™ classes. This is a workbook, not just a book to read. What you **know** when you finish reading this book won't be nearly as important to you or to your children as what you **do** when you finish this book. If you read the book, you will undoubtedly gain some new information, insight and understanding. If you do the exercises, you'll have the strongest foundation for putting your insight and understanding into practice.

*If you **do** read the whole book without stopping to do the exercises, I hope you will reread it and do them. It will be the difference between the experience of reading a bread recipe and that of baking and tasting the bread.

Your experience of **Connection Parenting** will be even richer if you bring other parents together and meet weekly to read and discuss the seven chapters as a group. Through learning Connection Parenting together, your group becomes your community of connection-parenting support.

I hope that the book provides not only information and inspiration to support you in building strong bonds with your children, but also validation and appreciation for the "connection" parenting you are already doing.

May *Connection Parenting* bring more understanding, love, joy, and connection to your relationships with children.

With my love and caring,

~ Pam Leo

Introduction

Why do some children grow up to become a Gandhi and others a Hitler?

What happens from birth to adulthood that determines that difference?

The Missing Connection

A consistent, loving connection with at least one adult is essential to create the healthy, strong parent-child bond that children need to thrive.

There is, and has been for many years, an abundance of well-documented research on what conditions help children thrive. Research shows that a secure bond with at least one adult is vital to the brain development that determines children's optimal physical, psychological, emotional, and spiritual wellbeing.

Why do we spend time and money to do research and then not disseminate the results of that research?

Parents are not told that our most important job is to secure and maintain a healthy, strong parent-child bond. This critical information, about the conditions that children need to thrive, has not made its way into the media. Parents hear far more about what new product to buy that will hold their babies than they do about the importance of holding their babies in their arms. What our children need most, money can't buy. Our children need human connection. A healthy, strong parent-child bond, created through consistent, loving connection, is essential to our children's wellbeing and optimal development. This bond is also the key to our effectiveness as parents.

Many children are in crisis. Parents are reading parenting books and taking classes. Many of us are looking for answers because we are struggling. Parenting has always been work, but it hasn't always been a struggle. Our grandparents and great-grandparents didn't read books on parenting or take parenting classes. Did they already know about bonding? No. Our great-grandparents didn't know about bonding either. It was not what they **knew** that made parenting different for them, it was **how they lived.**

In our great-grandparents' day, children's need for human connection was met naturally by a lifestyle that supported a strong parent-child bond. Babies were born at home, they were breast-fed, and spent their early years at home. The mother-infant bond and parent-child connection was not compromised by separation. Parents' and children's lives were more connected.

Our lifestyle has changed dramatically. Today most babies are born in the hospital and are bottle-fed. This early compromise to connection is compounded by the reduced amount of time parents and children spend together. Many infants and young children spend long days away from their mothers and fathers.

The stressful pace of modern living, the loss of extended family support, and the ever-increasing amount of time adults and children spend with television and computers have further weakened the parent-child connection.

Because that vital parent-child bond grew naturally and was not created consciously, when our lifestyle changed we were unaware that those changes were eroding the parent-child connection essential to our children's wellbeing. Even though the adults didn't know something was missing, the children did. Children's unmet need for connection began to show as behavior problems.

Instead of addressing these behavior problems by asking, "What is not right for our children? Some adults asked, "What's wrong with our children?" Rather than looking for the cause of children's behavior, they focused on finding ways to change or control children's behavior. The answer they found to controlling children's problem behaviors was authoritarian parenting, control through coercion. Time has shown that coercion increased behavior problems instead of solving them.

Meanwhile, other adults asked a different question about the behavior problems, and they found a different answer. Children, like all living things, do not thrive when their needs are not met. If a seedling isn't growing well, we look at the growing conditions. We ask, "Is it getting enough sunlight? Is the drainage adequate?" When we get the plant's growing conditions right, the plant thrives. When we get human growing conditions right, children thrive.

The strong bond that once grew naturally must be cultivated now. It was changing how we lived that weakened the parent-child bond. Now it demands changing how we live to strengthen the bond. There is a growing population of parents who are adapting their lifestyle to create conditions that meet their children's need for more human connection.

The parenting practices that create the secure connection infants and toddlers need for a healthy, strong parent-child bond are now known as attachment parenting. Attachment parenting promotes natural childbirth and keeping babies in human contact through breastfeeding, wearing babies in slings, co-sleeping, and caregiver constancy in the early years. My work on strengthening the bond with children of all ages, through providing consistent, loving connection, is becoming known as Connection Parenting.

Connection Parenting is not a "new" way of parenting; rather, it is a return to providing the parent-child connection that children need. We cannot go back to the old lifestyle where parents and children were connected naturally by how they lived. So, let's go forward and intentionally create the conditions for connection in our new lifestyle and provide our children with the strong parent-child bond they need to thrive.

What is Connection Parenting?

Connection parenting is parenting through connection instead of coercion, through love instead of fear.

The parenting model that most of us grew up with was authoritarian parenting, which is based on fear. Some grew up with permissive parenting, which is also based on fear. Authoritarian parenting is based on the child's fear of losing the parent's love. Permissive parenting is based on the parent's fear of losing the child's love.

Connection Parenting promotes parenting practices that create and maintain a healthy, strong parent-child bond. Creating a strong bond is our primary work as parents and the key to our children's optimal human development. Children survive without a strong bond, but they don't thrive.

Both authoritarian parenting and permissive parenting are reactive. Connection Parenting is proactive. We do not focus on ways to discipline children when their unmet need for connection results in uncooperative or unacceptable behavior. Connection Parenting focuses on maintaining the consistent, loving connection that meets children's need for a strong parent-child bond.

Most of us grew up with parenting based on coercion or threats. While threats of punishment or consequences accomplish temporary compliance, threats create disconnection and undermine the parent-child bond. Coercion is a quick fix, like the donut tire we use until we can replace our flat with a real tire. We wouldn't head out for a long journey on a donut tire. Parenting is a long journey.

Parenting through connection instead of coercion challenges our beliefs about what parents are "supposed" to do with children. Many parents say they wish children came with an instruction manual because they often find parenting advice confusing and contradictory. One expert or book says to do one thing, and another says to do the opposite.

Advice that promotes coercion is counterproductive to effective parenting. The level of cooperation parents get from children is usually equal to the level of connection children feel with their parents. Coercion weakens connection and undermines the strength of your bond. Whenever you feel confused about parenting advice, ask yourself, "If I follow this advice, will I create a connection or a disconnection with my child?"

Connection Parenting is not an instruction manual that teaches you how to control your child's behavior. It is a book about children's need for connection and the importance of meeting that need. Children have many of the same needs and also many different needs. Children are the experts on their needs, and they are always trying to tell us what they need. Connection Parenting is about listening to children and finding our best ways to meet their needs.

Parenting through connection is not a quick fix. Building a strong bond with a child takes time, effort, and commitment. Do you remember the little pig that built his house out of brick? He put in the time and did the work to build a strong house. When the big bad wolf came along, he couldn't blow it in like he could the houses of straw and sticks. If our children are to survive and thrive, they need adults who take the time and do the work to build a strong bond.

Parents also need that strong bond. Our parenting effectiveness is in direct proportion to the strength of the connection we have with our child. When we have a strong connection, we don't have to resort to coercion.

*We parent through connection, not coercion,
because we build strong bonds only by connecting.*

Parenting Through Love Instead of Fear

Can you imagine threatening your partner
or good friend by counting "One... two... three..."
if he or she did not do what you wanted?

One of the biggest issues in schools today is "bullying." Parents and teachers struggle daily with how to stop this behavior. Without realizing it, adults teach bullying behavior to children by modeling it when they use the threat of their physical size or power to make children do things. This is parenting through coercion.

When I hear a parent counting "One... two" at a young child, I always wonder what the parent told the child would happen if the parent gets to three. Is it the threat of a spanking, being yelled at, or being put in time-out? Perhaps it is the threat of abandonment (I am going without you) or the withdrawal of love and approval.

Whatever the threat may be, I rarely hear "three." As intended, the threat compels the child to do whatever the parent wants. Parents use threats to get children to cooperate because that was what adults modeled when we were growing up. Most of us are familiar with the phrase "or else." We did what we were told out of fear, even if we didn't know what the "or else" would be. While counting appears to be a magic form of discipline, there is no magic in threats. Children know that adults are bigger and more powerful than they are and comply in self-defense.

If the only way we can get children to do what we ask is by intimidating them, how will we get them to do as we ask when we are no longer bigger and more powerful? Ask the parents of any teenager if counting still works. Not only do threats no longer work, children learn to use threats to make others do what they want.

Parents often see uncooperative behavior as a challenge to their authority. Once we understand that uncooperative behavior is a communication of a child's unmet need, a hurt, or the response to an adult's unrealistic expectation, we do not have to take the behavior so personally. Parents and children both have needs. Children who are deeply absorbed in play will not want to stop playing and go with us to the bank or the store. When an adult needs to do one thing and a child needs to do another, there is competition to get their needs met. This competition turns into a power struggle when we use the power of fear instead of the power of love.

Our bond or connection with a child is our most powerful parenting tool. We create a strong bond over time when we lovingly and consistently meet a child's early needs. Threats communicate, "What you think, feel, want, or need is not important." Threats undermine the parent-child bond. When we learn to relate in ways that show children that their needs and feelings matter, we strengthen the bond and avoid power struggles.

Lack of resources is the most common reason for competing to get our needs met. If we had more resources, we would not have to bring the child to the bank or the store because there would be someone else to stay with the child. As long as there is lack of resources, there will be competition between parents and children to get their needs met. Until we figure out how to bring more resources into our lives, we have to find ways to cooperate and collaborate if we are to stop teaching children to be bullies.

We can use conflict resolution skills in our daily interactions with children. Just as children learn bullying from what adults model, they can learn conflict resolution and problem solving skills instead.

Very young children learn conflict resolution when we model it. We can teach an older child to find another toy to exchange with their younger sibling instead of snatching their toy back. When two children want the same toy at the same time, we can help them "problem solve" a solution.

When there is a power struggle because the parent wants to run an errand and the child wants to stay home, we can say, "Let's problem solve to find a way for both of us to get what we need." Maybe the child could take the toy in the car or perhaps the errand could wait until tomorrow.

When we are ready to leave the playground and the child wants to stay longer, we can offer a compromise of staying five more minutes and having more fun when we get home. Often, it is not that the child doesn't want to leave as much as it is that she doesn't want the fun to end. We teach children that everyone's needs are important by honoring their needs. From our example, they learn to honor other's needs.

We may not have the time or the resources to meet a child's need. Sometimes, even after we offer a compromise, the child is still unable to cooperate. Then, we communicate that parents have needs too. If setting the limit still makes the child unhappy, we listen to those feelings before we move forward.

It is never okay to tell young children that you will leave without them. Threatening abandonment terrifies young children. When a child has a tantrum about leaving, the tantrum may not be about leaving. The disappointment of leaving may be the last straw that unleashes an accumulation of little frustrations. The child may need to empty out the stresses of the day. A child can move forward more readily when we say, "I know you're sad and it's okay to cry," instead of "Stop that crying or I'll give you something to cry about!" When children finish crying, they feel better and are more able to cooperate.

Children are delightful to be with when we meet their needs and nothing is hurting them. Whenever a child responds negatively to a reasonable request, we look for the hidden hurt or the unmet need. Once we acknowledge everyone's needs, we can work on problem solving.

I have learned to say, "When you behave that way I know something is wrong. We love each other and people who love each other don't treat each other this way. Can you tell me what you need or what's hurting you?" If I can remember to stop and ask that one simple question, it changes the whole context of the power struggle. That question communicates, "I love you, and what you feel and need matters to me."

Sometimes there isn't a way for both people to get what they need. However, not getting what we need is easier to bear if we are treated in a way that allows us to keep our dignity. Threatening or counting at a child communicates, "I am bigger and more powerful, and you'd better do as I say, or I'm going to hurt you." When a big kid says to a smaller one, "Do what I say, or I'm going to hurt you," we call it bullying. When an adult communicates the same message to a child by counting, we call it discipline.

Treating children in ways that take away their dignity teaches them to do the same to others. If we want kids to stop bullying, we have to stop bullying kids. The power of fear is easy and quick, but short-lived. The power of love requires more work and takes longer, but children never outgrow its influence.

The children who now depend on us to meet their needs while they are young will one day be the adults we depend on to meet our needs when we are old. They will be able to give only what they have received. Let's parent through connection instead of coercion, through love instead of fear.

Basic Premises of Meeting Children's Needs Through Connection Parenting

- The greatest emotional need of every child is to bond securely to at least one other human being.

- Our most important task as parents is to secure and maintain a healthy, strong parent-child bond.

- Maintaining connection is the key to loving, effective parenting and to our children's optimal human development.

- Parents are always doing the best they can with the information, resources, and support they have at any given moment.

- The level of cooperation parents get from their children is usually equal to the level of connection children feel with their parents.

- What children want and need most is to be with us and to do what we do.

- Children want to be with us to maintain connection.

- Children want to do what we do because we are their models.

- All behaviors are need-driven. We do what we do to get our needs met.

- When children's needs are met and nothing is hurting them, they are delightful. When children are not being delightful, their behavior is telling us about something they need.

- At times, children are not able to identify or communicate with words what they need or what hurts. Children communicate by acting out their needs and hurts through their behavior (thus acting-out behavior).

- We can't teach children to behave better by making them feel worse. Children behave better when they feel better.

- We can learn to decode children's behavior and respond to their needs, instead of react to their behaviors.

- It takes the same amount of time and attention to meet children's needs as it does to deal with the behaviors caused by their unmet needs.

- The only conflict that exists between parents and children is between the strategies that we use to get our needs met.

- Whether we are unconsciously raising our children the way our parents raised us or we are consciously trying to do the exact opposite, the way we parent is influenced by the way we were parented.

- Parenting never used to be and was never intended by nature to be a one or two person job. Families work best when everyone's needs are met. It does take a village to meet the needs of children and parents.

- We will never become perfect parents who raise perfect children, but we can learn how to make it better for our children, for us, and for our world.

- It is never too late to create a stronger connection with our children.

Chapter 1
Connecting With Ourselves

We did the best with what we knew;
now we know more so we can do better. - Oprah

The more we learn, the more we expect of ourselves. One rule in Connection Parenting workshops is not to use this information to beat yourself up for what you didn't know or couldn't do. Making ourselves wrong for not doing it right doesn't serve our children or us.

When we read a new parenting book or take a class, we often feel guilty for not already knowing or always doing what we learn. It is important to make the distinction between guilt and regret. Guilt is what we feel when we knew better and didn't act on what we knew. Regret is the sadness we feel when we learn something new that we wish we had known earlier. Making this distinction between guilt and regret is important as we embark on learning some different ways of parenting.

Most of us know what we need to do to be physically healthy, yet we don't practice what we know all the time. Some days we eat healthy foods and some days we eat unhealthy foods. One week we exercise regularly and the next week we don't exercise at all. If we grew up eating healthy foods and getting regular exercise, it is easier to do that consistently as adults. If we didn't grow up eating healthy foods and getting regular exercise, we have difficulty forming those new healthful habits as adults. It is easier to walk a beaten path than it is to break a new trail.

Whatever we experienced as children comes automatically to us as adults. If we are trying to parent our children differently from the way we were parented, the new ways challenge us. Just as we will be healthier if we eat well and exercise some of the time, our parenting will be more nurturing if we practice connection parenting some of the time.

The more often we remember to parent through connection, the stronger our parent-child bond will be. The stronger the bond, the better able our children will be to weather the times when we parent in less nurturing ways.

The parents who attend my Connection Parenting series want to become the best parents they can be. Parents are always doing the best they can, at any given moment, with the information, resources, and support they have. I've never met a parent who woke up in the morning and said, "What could I do today to really mess up my kids?"

There is always a gap between learning a new way and being able to do it consistently. Scott Noelle, parenting coach and author of articles on conscious, holistic parenting, describes this as, "The gap between the healthy parenting ideals you embrace intellectually and what you're capable of doing in the here and now."

Becoming better parents means we will always be learning. It also means we will be living in the gap sometimes between what we are learning and what we can do. The more we learn about healthier parenting, the more we will live in the "gap." As we strive to become more loving to our children, we must also strive to be more loving to ourselves.

> ## Ancora Imparo - I am still learning.
> ### - Michelangelo

Parenting practices are cultural. The way we parent is influenced not only by how we were parented, but also by the parenting practices observed in our culture. The United States has become a weak bonding culture. We don't have to observe weak bonding parenting practices just because that is what our culture dictates as "normal." We can choose the healthy, strong-bond parenting practices our children are programmed biologically to expect and need for optimal human development.

Every parent I have ever known has wanted life to be better for their children than it was for them. Many parents regret that they did not have the information or support to practice connection parenting earlier. In Connection Parenting workshops, the feedback I get most often is, "I wish I'd had this information from the beginning." I, too, wish I'd had this information from the beginning.

It is never too late to strengthen our connection with our children. Every moment is a new opportunity to strengthen the bond.

Where did we learn how to be a parent?

Parenting our children is the most important and challenging job any of us will ever have. Unlike all other important jobs, parenting is the one for which we get no formal preparation, education, or training.

With the help of the parents in Connection Parenting classes, I created the following exercises to empower you to learn and consciously choose parenting practices that will strengthen your bond with your children.

Preparation for Connection Parenting

REMINDER: Although it will be tempting to only read or even skip these exercises and keep going, I implore you to take the time to do them. Write them down, because all the "**light bulbs**" will be in your words, not in mine.

* I recommend that you write the exercises in a special, permanent parenting journal that you can add to over the years and track your progress.

My Parenting Goals:
What do you hope to give and not give to your children?

To get the most out of this book you need to identify your specific parenting goals.

Draw a line down the middle of a piece of paper or on a page in your parenting journal.

In the left column, write a list of what you want for your children. (Anything that nurtures—unconditional love, encouragement, self-esteem, or confidence.) This is the nurturing list.

In the right column, write a list of what you don't want for your children. (Anything that hurts—yelling, spanking, etc.) This is the hurts list.

Your Parenting Inheritance:

What did you get or not get from your parents? The more conscious we become about how our parents' methods affected us, the more conscious we become of how our parenting affects our children.

When you've completed the two lists, put a check mark next to anything in the nurturing column that you got as a child.

Put a check mark next to any thing in the hurts column that you got as a child.

What do you notice about your checkmarks in each column? Which column has the most check marks?

*IMPORTANT NOTE: Our parents were doing the best they could with the information, resources and support they had. Every generation of parents softens what they got for their children. If what we got was harsh, imagine what our parents got. We parent our children best when we can forgive, heal, and not pass on hurts.

My Parenting Strengths:

The nurturing you got will support you in providing what you want for your children. Use the check-marked statements in the nurturing column to begin a list of your parenting strengths.

My Parenting Challenges:

Begin a list of parenting challenges with the unchecked statements in the nurturing column. The nurturing you did not get will be challenging to give. You need to learn actively how to do that kind of nurturing because you did not have a model of how to do that for your children.

More Parenting Challenges:

The hurts you check-marked in the right column are models you had of how to treat children. You don't want to pass those hurts on to your children. Add the check-marked statements in the hurts column to your parenting challenges list. Where you have emotional hurts, you have emotional healing work to do. *We are less likely to pass on our hurts when we do our own healing work.*

The next exercise requires the participation of another person. You can choose your parenting partner, another parent, or a close friend. The purpose of this exercise is to bring your unconscious parent training to a conscious level so you can choose which parts of that training you intentionally want to repeat and which parts you want to replace.

Mini-biography:

Take turns sharing your mini-biography by doing a listening partnership. When one person is telling their biography, the listener simply listens and does not interrupt by commenting or asking questions.

• Tell your name, age, and where you grew up.

• Tell how many children were in your family and your birth position: only child, twin, oldest, youngest, middle etc.

• Tell the story of your parents, keeping in mind that we can take neither credit nor blame for their story, it's simply their story. Example: My parents are still married after 40 years. They were divorced when I was two. My father was an alcoholic. My mother died when I was eight.

• Tell about discipline in your family—your own and your siblings. Recall one fond memory from your childhood— vacation, holiday, special time with a grandparent etc.

• During the coming week, following the mini-biography exercise, notice what you do and say as a parent.

• What do you do and say that is the same as the way you were parented?

• What did your parents do and say that you find yourself repeating, but want to do differently?

• Add these to your parenting challenges list.

• Add the following to your parenting strengths list:

• What do you do and say that you have already consciously chosen to do differently than your parents did?

• What did your parents do or say that you have consciously chosen to repeat and pass on to your children?

• What do you do and say as a parent that you feel good about?

Take a few minutes to appreciate your strengths.

Your lists of parenting goals, strengths, and challenges are your maps for the parenting journey. **Connection Parenting** is your guide.

PUZZLE PIECES:

 When Your Kids Push Your Buttons by Bonnie Harris

 ScreamFree Parenting - Raising your Kids by Keeping Your Cool by Hal Edward Runkel

 Don't Let Your Emotions Run Your Life - How Dialectical Behavior Therapy Can Put You In Control by Scott E.Spradlin, MA

Connection Parenting Terms and Tools

Throughout this book, I use the terms connection and disconnection. I define those terms as follows:

Connection - feeling loved and listened to.
Disconnection - feeling hurt and unheard.

Many parents who attend my classes say that they are there to get new parenting "tools." In Connection Parenting, there are only two tools.

The goal of Connection Parenting is to meet proactively children's need for connection. Whenever the optimal level of connection gets too low, children communicate their need for more connection through their behavior. When a child's behavior challenges us, we use tool #1.

TOOL # 1: Connection

Provide children with a consistent, loving connection through eye contact, loving touch, respect, listening, and spending time working and playing together.

Whenever we question how to respond to a child's behavior, we ask ourselves, "Is this response connection or coercion?" Look for a way to respond to the behavior without creating a disconnection. Connect before you correct.

TOOL # 2: Reconnection

Sometimes a child's behavior pushes our buttons and we react before we connect. We can tell when our reaction has caused disconnection. A child who feels hurt and/or unheard will either:

Attack – cry or scream

   Or

Retreat – won't make eye contact with, won't talk to us, and rejects our touch

As soon as we realize our reaction has created a disconnection we reconnect with tool #2.

The 3 R's of reconnection are:

Rewind – acknowledge our hurtful behavior ("What I said was hurtful")

Repair – apologize and let the child know he did not deserve our behavior

Replay – respond with love and listening

We will always know when connection is re-established. When children feel connected, they make eye contact with us, they talk to us, and they welcome our touch.

You now have the Connection Parenting tools. However, tools are only useful when we also have the skills to use them. The rest of this book is devoted to supporting you in developing and practicing the skills to use the Connection Parenting tools to maintain connection and build the strong bonds children need to thrive.

Before you read Chapter Two
Getting the most from this book

The lists you created in Chapter One will direct your use of the material in the rest of this book. You will be asked to refer to your list of parenting goals (what you do and do not want to give to your children) in other chapters.

The seven chapters of this book are organized to replicate the seven sessions of Connection Parenting™ "Meeting the Needs of Children" workshop series. The classes meet for two hours each week and participants have a week between each topic to put what they have learned into practice, and return and share their experiences. If you are reading this book with a book group that meets once a week, I recommend that you do a chapter a week. If you are reading this book on your own, I recommend doing no more than a chapter a day to get the most from each chapter.

We learn in three ways: explanation, example, and experience.

The explanations and examples in this book teach about connecting with children. Learning from experience will come from practicing connecting with children. This chapter explains why we need to treat children with the same respect we expect. The examples of the difference between treating children with respect or disrespect explain why disrespect causes disconnection and respect creates connection.

The explanations and examples in this book are from Connection Parenting classes. The part of the Connection

Parenting class that I cannot replicate in this book is the check-in. Each week, class participants hear how other parents, in other circumstances, interpreted and implemented the information from the previous session. One of the advantages of reading this book with a group, or with at least one other person, is that you get to experience the wonderful sharing, feedback, and support.

Chapter 2
Connecting with Children through Respecting Children

Children learn what they live.
- Dorothy Law Nolte

I am embarrassed to say I had been teaching my "Meeting the Needs of Children" parenting series for many years before I discovered the work of Joseph Chilton Pearce through his book, **Magical Child.** Even though I was teaching parents to meet children's emotional needs, I wasn't telling them **why** it is so important. It was through Pearce's work that I made the connection about connection. Understanding the vital importance of the parent-child bond pulled all the puzzle pieces together.

Meeting children's emotional needs creates and maintains the essential bond they need to thrive. The bond is a child's consistent, loving connection with at least one other person. Studies show that many infants and young children, in orphanages, whose physical needs were met, "failed to thrive," or even died from lack of touch, attention, and connection.

Children's emotional needs are as important as their physical needs. Those orphans died from non-organic failure-to-thrive because they had no consistent loving connection with at least one adult. If infants can die from the lack of a consistent loving connection, and strongly bonded children thrive, might that explain why children with a weak bond survive physically but do not thrive?

One of children's most basic emotional needs is to be treated with respect. The foundation of Connection Parenting is treating children with respect. Children need to be treated with the same respect that we expect if we are to meet their need for connection. Disrespect hurts. Hurts cause disconnection. Disconnection undermines the strength of the parent-child bond.

For too long, children have been treated as second-class citizens, as "less than" adults. The idea of treating children with the same respect we expect feels strange to parents who grew up hearing "children should be seen and not heard." I have asked many parents who grew up hearing that phrase, what it meant to them as children. Most say it meant that they were supposed to be quiet and how they felt or what they had to say didn't matter.

Adults often make the mistake of thinking that, because children are smaller, and have less information, and less experience, they don't have the same feelings we have. Children do have the same feelings, and they are more tender and vulnerable. The same words or actions that hurt our feelings and make us feel disrespected feel the same way to children. Dignity is not something we acquire when we become adults. All of us are born with human dignity. The same words or actions that take away our dignity also take away children's dignity.

One of the most common complaints I hear about children "today" is that they don't treat anyone or any thing with respect. How can children give respect without first receiving it? Children are not born being disrespectful; that behavior is learned. Children imitate parents, family members, friends, caregivers, teachers, and television. The more children are out in the world, the more models they are exposed to. We can't keep children from ever seeing models of the kind of behavior we don't want them to imitate, but we can be more selective of which models we expose them to, especially on television.

We cannot expect children to understand and practice the Golden Rule if we treat them in ways that we would not want to be treated. The wisdom "what goes around, comes around," and "as you sow, so shall you reap" applies to how we treat children. It behooves every adult who wishes respect, to treat children respectfully. Whether children grow up under our roof or not, they live in the same world we do, and their behavior impacts our lives.

If you question whether your words to a child are disrespectful, ask yourself, "Would I say those words, in that tone of voice, to my good friend?" If not, it was disrespectful.

In class, I read a brilliant piece by Erma Bombeck entitled, "Treat Friends, Kids The Same." Bombeck imagines having friends over for dinner and saying to them those phrases that many of us heard growing up.

"Shut the door. Were you born in a barn?"

"I didn't work over a hot stove all day to have you nibble like some bird."

"Sit up straight or your spine will grow that way."

Parents roar with laughter at the thought of speaking to their friends that way, and then realize it is just as disrespectful to say those things to children. Treating children with the same respect we would give our friends doesn't mean we should treat children as adults, or that we should be permissive, or never get angry.

Most of the disrespectful things adults say to children are so automatic, we have already said them before we realize it. Human beings are like tape recorders. Every word we hear is recorded permanently in our subconscious. Adults carry "recordings" of the disrespectful words they heard as children. When a child's behavior pushes our buttons, our recordings "play" and we find ourselves repeating what we heard as children. Have any parents not heard themselves say their parents' words to their children?

Children have never been very good at listening to their elders, but they have never failed to imitate them.
– James Baldwin

Ninety-five percent of what children learn comes from what adults model. Children are mirrors; they reflect back to us all that we say and do. Whenever adults speak, we are role models for the children in our presence. Children record every word we say to them or around them. Every time we are disrespectful to a child, we are modeling how to be disrespectful.

Children do what we do, not what we tell them to do. When we treat children with disrespect, they learn to be disrespectful. We teach respect by modeling it and by giving children the same respect we expect. The language we grew up hearing is the language we learned to speak.

Ironically, adults often try to teach children to be respectful by treating them disrespectfully. When adults instruct children by criticizing, lecturing, shaming, ridiculing, giving orders, screaming, threatening, and hitting, it hurts children. When human beings are hurt emotionally, our thinking shuts down. When a child's thinking is shut down, he can't learn what the adult intended to teach him to do or not to do. He can only record and imitate what is modeled. If we are committed to maintaining connection with our children, we must acknowledge, expose, and work on eliminating treating children with disrespect.

We must become the people we want our children to be.

*- Joseph Chilton Pearce, author of **Magical Child***

Treating children with respect requires a change of heart that comes only from a major shift in how we view children and how we define respect. Modeling the behavior we want children to learn is the respectful way to teach them. If we expect children to have manners, to share, to apologize, to be honest, kind, respectful, and loving, we must do and be those. Learning to teach children through conscious, intentional modeling takes time, practice, and our willingness to see and change our behavior.

Parents are the primary models in the early years. Children need adults who model the behavior they expect. When a child doesn't behave in the ways we expect, we ask ourselves, "Am I providing a model of the behavior I expect and will accept from my children?"

Remember: Our children record and imitate all that we say and do. Learning to teach by intentional modeling is simple, but not easy. Stopping our old tapes from playing is difficult. While we are training ourselves to be as respectful to children as we are to adults, our buttons will get pushed. Our old disrespect tapes will play and create disconnection.

We reconnect by using tool # 2 – Rewind, Repair, and Replay. Saying, "rewind" is an acknowledgment that we caught ourselves communicating in a disrespectful way. We repair by apologizing. Then we replay the scene by treating the child respectfully.

When we model correcting our behavior with rewind, repair, and replay, then we can remind children to "rewind" when they speak or behave in disrespectful or unacceptable ways. They will know from our example that they, too, can reconnect by rewinding, repairing, and replaying their way of speaking or behaving. When we give children the same respect that we expect, we model respect and we maintain connection.

Walking our Talk: If we choose to remind children to be respectful by saying, "rewind" when they are disrespectful, we must give children permission to remind us to rewind when we are disrespectful.

Practicing Connection Parenting

Some of the disrespectful ways adults treat children have been said and done to children for so long, we are often unaware that they are disrespectful.

When you were a child did any adult ever:

• Prompt you to say please and thank you?

• Insist that you say you were sorry?

• Force you to share your toys?

• Demand that you to hug or kiss family members or friends when you didn't want to?

• Give orders instead of requests?

• Talk about you in front of you as if you were not there?

Can you remember how it felt to be treated that way?

As children, we believed we deserved the way we were treated. The way we were treated was our model of how to treat children.

Now, as an adult, do you ever:

- Prompt children to say please and thank you?

- Insist children say sorry?

- Force children to share their toys?

- Demand that children hug or kiss family members or friends when they don't want to?

- Give children orders instead of requests?

- Talk about children in front of them as if they were not there?

When considering these questions, many parents squirm in their seats because most of us have treated children this way at one time or another. I know I have, and sometimes still do when my buttons get pushed and I don't catch my old coercion "tapes" in time. Then I have to rewind, repair, and replay.

How we treat them is what we teach them.

When we model using coercion, we teach children to use coercion. We have heard a child say to another child, "You're not the boss of me." Our job as parents is to be our children's leaders, not their bosses. We want our children to follow our leadership out of trust, love, and respect, not out of fear.

Examples of Treating Children with the Same Respect We Expect

We maintain connection with children and strengthen our bond when we practice the Golden Rule and give children the same respect we would give our friends.

We teach children to be courteous by modeling good manners.

Prompting children to say please and thank you embarrasses them. We don't say, "What do you say?" or "What's the magic word?" to our friends, but children hear it all the time. Do we **always** say please and thank-you to children and each other? If not, we are modeling that sometimes you say it and sometimes you don't. Children then imitate the model of sometimes you say it and sometimes you don't. If we expect children always to say please and thank-you, we model always saying please and thank-you to them and to each other.

One of the hardest parts of teaching manners by modeling courtesy instead of instructing children to be courteous is that we feel embarrassed when our children forget. We fear that people will think we are not teaching our children manners. Whenever children don't remember to say thank you to someone, we simply thank the person. The person is appreciated and children see our model of courtesy.

We teach children to apologize by saying, "I'm sorry," to children and to each other.

When children know they have done something wrong, they experience a loss of dignity. Insisting that children say they are sorry increases their loss of dignity. Losing dignity is an emotional hurt. When children feel hurt they cannot think well. When they cannot think well, they cannot learn. Children need our support to regain their dignity and to figure out a way to make amends. Instead of insisting children say sorry, we help them think of a way to make amends. (Getting a cold cloth for a boo-boo, gluing a broken toy)

We teach generosity by modeling sharing.

Forcing children to share their toys is coercion. When we use our size and power to force children to share, they comply out of fear, not generosity. Expecting young children to share is an unrealistic adult expectation.

Children learn to share by seeing models of sharing. Even though we do model sharing many things with children, we don't model sharing toys. We teach sharing toys by modeling sharing toys. Instead of always buying toys for your children, try having your own toy box and sharing your toys with your children and those who come to visit.

Adults claim the right to decide which of their possessions they will or will not allow children to use. Children learn to say, "This is mine, you may not use it," from the model of adults saying, "This is mine. You may not use it." That message teaches children that when we own something, we get to decide about it. If they own something, they expect to be able to decide about it. Being respectful means that we respect children's right to decide about their things. This means being more selective about what we give to children and what we buy for our own toy box or for the family. Most children own more toys than they know what to do with. Children don't have to own toys to have use of them.

As with manners, we fear that others will think we don't teach our children to share if we don't force them to share. Sharing our toys and inviting children to bring some toys they will not be forced to share demonstrates that we choose to teach sharing in a different way.

It is an adult's job to meet a child's emotional needs. It is not a child's job to meet an adult's emotional needs.

Did you ever have to hug or kiss a relative even when you did not want to? Do you remember what that felt like? If adults are to be respectful to children, we offer affection instead of demanding it. Demanding that children hug or kiss family members or a friend does not teach children to be affectionate. It teaches children that they don't get to decide about their bodies.

We offer affection by saying, "I have a hug for you, would you like to have it?" Sometimes children say no just because they can. Usually children accept with delight if they have a bond with the person who is making the offer.

When grandparents, other relatives, or friends request or demand affection from our children, one way we respect our children's feelings, and protect them from "having to" fill an adult's need for affection, is to offer ourselves in their place. "I guess Sammy doesn't have any hugs or kisses today, but I do." If we aren't kissing great-grandma goodbye, we have no business demanding that our children must. If we expect children to be affectionate to others, we model being affectionate to others.

We don't have to hurt an adult's feelings to respect a child's feelings.

We can be pro-active by talking to children and brainstorming ideas that protect everyone's feelings, before we visit people we know may ask for affection. Sometimes children feel fine about giving a "high-five" or throwing kisses if we talk about it ahead of time. The ham radio term for hugs and kisses is 88. We often say "88" for quick good-byes, phone good-byes, and good-byes for people who request or demand affection.

Children respond to invitations

We feel diminished when someone is giving us an order or command rather than making a request. Children feel the same way. We get more cooperation from children with an invitation than an order. When we give orders, we create a disconnection.

Children want to be with us and to do what we do.

The most "magic" word I know is "Let's." "Let's pick up the toys." "Let's go brush our teeth." "Let's leave our muddy boots by the door." Let's say let's. It works!

The only time "let's" doesn't gain cooperation is when there is already a disconnection. Then we need to reconnect before we say "let's." When a child refuses to cooperate with a respectful, reasonable, request or invitation there is a hurt somewhere that needs addressing before we can reconnect.

Include the child in the conversation when we need to speak to another adult about a child in the child's presence.

We start talking about children in front of them when they are babies and can't speak for themselves. Then we forget to stop doing that when they are old enough to speak for themselves. Can you even imagine talking to your friend Ted about your friend, Polly, as if she were not standing right there? Adults do this to children all the time.

As a childcare provider, I was expected to tell parents about the child's day when they picked up their child. I learned to be respectful to children by including the child in the conversation. I would say, "Let's tell Mom/Dad about our day." Sometimes the child would join the conversation and sometimes she would say, "You tell," and run off to play. Either way, I was being more respectful.

We must become the change we want to see in the world
- Gandhi

Parenting is work no matter how we do it.

Parents often say, "But coercion works." Yes, it works, but for how long and at what cost? If children do what we ask or expect only because we coerce them, we will always have to be there to give instructions and orders. Teaching through modeling takes longer than teaching through coercion. Modeling alone will not produce the behaviors and values we expect. It is having a strong bond with their model that causes children to want to behave in ways that maintain connection. Children with a strong bond, who have learned from our modeling, are more likely to do what we expect without being told.

Coercion parenting is a quick fix but doesn't build a strong bond. Connection parenting takes more time, but it builds a strong bond. We either do the work of creating a strong bond when they are younger or we will do the work of dealing with behaviors caused by a weak bond when they are older. It takes the same amount of time and attention to meet children's need for connection as it does to deal with behaviors caused by their unmet needs.

Treating children with respect maintains connection and strengthens the bond. Coercion may work when children are little, but when they are big we need something much stronger than coercion. *Connection is stronger than coercion.*

Treating children with respect means adopting new ways of treating and talking to children. It takes time to form new habits. During that time when our buttons are pushed we often react and resort to coercion. Whenever we do, we use tool #2. We rewind, repair, and replay to reconnect.

In your Parenting Journal:

Refer back to your list of parenting goals. As you read them, do you see anything on your list that treating children with more respect would support your efforts to give children the nurturing you want to give them?

Refer back to your list of parenting challenges. Do you see anything on the list that treating children with more respect would support your efforts in avoiding the hurts?

 Escape From Childhood by John Holt

 When I Am Little Again and The Child's Right To Respect by Janusz Korczak

 Magical Child by Joseph Chilton Pearce

Chapter 3
Connecting through Listening to Children's Feelings

It is our job to protect children from harm, but we cannot protect them from emotional hurts. Disappointment, frustration, fear, embarrassment, feeling left out, and loss are part of the human experience. While we cannot protect children from experiencing those emotional hurts, we can support children in healing from their hurts.

It is not our job to stop children from crying. Once we understand how children (and adults) naturally and spontaneously heal emotional hurts, we can support rather than thwart the healing process. Children heal their own hurts when they have the safety provided by adults who are willing to listen to their feelings.

Have you ever felt upset and had a friend listen without interrupting by giving advice or trying to fix it, while you talked, cried, and complained? Once you emptied out the hurt feelings, can you remember how much better and connected you felt to that friend? Children feel better and more connected to us when we listen to their feelings without interrupting, giving advice, or trying to fix it. Listening to children's feelings builds connection and strengthens the bond.

Healing Emotional Hurts

Human beings heal emotional hurts through the natural, spontaneous process of releasing the painful feelings that result from hurt. If you observe young children you will notice that they spontaneously cry when hurt, upset, or frightened. Research on human tears shows that the tears we cry of emotion contain stress hormones. Tears release pain and stress. Other ways we release emotional hurts and stress are screaming, raging, talking repeatedly about the hurt, shaking, laughing, perspiring, and yawning.

Without this information, parents and caregivers don't know what to do when a child cries or rages. If our attempts to comfort or fix the problem don't stop the crying, we become frustrated and even angry with the child. Children need adults to stay with them and support them while they release their pain instead of stopping them from crying. Interrupting the crying interferes with the natural healing process.

Why and How Adults Stop Children from Healing Emotional Hurts

Because our parents did not have this information, most of us grew up hearing, "There, there it's okay... don't cry. There's nothing to cry about. Don't be a sissy. Big boys don't cry. Stop that crying or I'll give you something to cry about!" If we grew up hearing those responses to our feelings, we carry those recordings and say the same phrases to our children when they cry or get angry.

Young children learn to shut down the emotional healing process when they get messages that it is not acceptable to express their painful feelings. These ten different responses close down children's emotional healing process:

• Invalidating – "There, there, there's nothing to cry about or be afraid of."

• Shaming – "Don't cry. Be a big boy/girl. Don't be a sissy. Don't be a baby."

• Threatening – "I'll give you something to cry about!"

• Placating or fixing it – "I'll get you a new one."

• Distraction – "Let's go get a cookie."

• Isolation – "Go to your room until you can stop crying."

• Ignoring – Unspoken or spoken, "I won't talk to you until you stop crying."

• Outdoing – "You think that's bad, listen to what happened to me."

• Guilting – "You have so much; you shouldn't be upset over this."

• Humoring – Child falls on the pavement, "Did you hurt that driveway?"

All of these responses give children a clear message: "Shut down the expression and release of your painful feelings."

If you are reading this book with a book reader's group, pick a partner and take turns telling what you recall being said when you were a young child and you were crying or angry. Take one minute for your telling, and then listen for one minute to your partner.

This is also important information to exchange with your parenting partner. It will help you understand why each of you responds the way you do to your children's crying and anger.

If you are not in a book group, make a journal entry that describes what you recall being said when you cried or got angry.

Most of us experienced some interference when we released our painful feelings, and it was usually gender-specific. It was somewhat acceptable for little girls to cry, but not to be angry. It wasn't "nice" or lady-like to express anger. It was somewhat acceptable for little boys to express anger, but not to cry, which was considered being a sissy or a crybaby. As a result, many grown women cry when they feel angry and many grown men get angry when they feel hurt, because those were the only permitted avenues of expression. Females get angry and males feel grief. Feelings are not gender-specific.

Storing Emotional Hurts

We need the attention of another person while we release our painful feelings. We need someone to listen to us. Children know this. Have you seen a child fall on the playground and then look around to see if anyone noticed? If no one acknowledges seeing the fall, he probably won't cry. He knows there is no one to listen. If someone does notice he fell, he may cry and cry. When there is a big cry over a little hurt, the tears are about more than this hurt.

- When emotional hurts occur and there is no one to listen, it doesn't feel safe to release the painful feelings.

- Children (and adults) store unreleased hurts.

- We store the tears that we don't cry.

- When someone cries, the crying may be about more than the current hurt.

- When someone listens, the current hurt triggers the release of stored hurts.

- When we invalidate children's feelings, they learn to stop trusting their feelings.

- We say, "Don't express your feelings." Children hear, "Don't feel your feelings."

- We say, "I can't accept your feelings;" children hear, "I can't accept you."

Children desperately need us to accept them. Rather than risk rejection for expressing their painful feelings, children learn to stop expressing their feelings.

Control Behaviors

Children learn to control the release of their feelings just as they learn bladder control. When children learn that it is not acceptable to release their bladders spontaneously in response to them being full, they develop control over those muscles so they can "hold it" until they make it to the appropriate place. When children learn that it is not acceptable to release their feelings, they develop the control to keep them inside.

In order to control the release of their feelings, children develop control behaviors like nail biting, hair twirling, and chewing on clothes, hair, and pencils. Young children have not had the time to develop much control over releasing their feelings. The smaller children are, the less capacity they have to store hurts. Typically, as children get older, they gain more control and have a greater capacity to store hurts.

However, some children release more often and more intensely than others do. A sensitive child experiences hurts at a deeper level than others do. His cup fills faster, and he needs to empty it more often. Children who release hurts often, have more hurts to release or simply may not be able to hold hurt inside for long. If you have a child who tantrums frequently and intensely you may have a "spirited" child.

Emotional Safety

Once children develop control behaviors, the only time they release their feelings is when they feel safe or when they have no more room inside to store them. Safety is the explanation for why people say children act "worst" with their parents. Whenever the safety is sufficient, the release of painful feelings is spontaneous. Parents are usually their children's "safe" place.

Children frequently hold in their hurts when they are away from their parents. Parents may hear glowing reports from others about how their child behaved all day, only to have their child erupt into a tantrum the moment they come home.

Safety is also the explanation for why children sometimes erupt into a tantrum in response to having had lots of loving attention. When we spend time connecting with children, they feel loved and safe. If there are hurts lurking inside, our loving attention provides the safe place that triggers release.

Parents feel frustrated when they have spent time and attention connecting with their child, and now the child is dredging up old hurts that feel like criticism. Please **remember** that part of connecting is creating the safety that allows children to release and heal the stored hurts that get in the way of connecting.

Safety has the same affect on adults. Adults are experts at holding in painful feelings. There could be an accident, an illness or a death, and we hold our feelings in until our safe person walks though the door, and then we fall apart.

Temper Tantrums

Having no more room to store hurt is the explanation for temper tantrums. A temper tantrum is spillover. Imagine that every child has a cup inside to store the unreleased hurts. The cup fills with unreleased hurts. Then one more hurt happens, and the child explodes with crying, anger, frustration, or rage. Our efforts to reason, comfort, or to fix are useless. We don't know why the child is behaving this way, and we don't know what to do. The hurt we did see didn't seem to warrant this intense response. The tantrum is the release of the accumulated hurts we didn't see.

Tantrums push our buttons. We may feel anxious, angry, or embarrassed. The child's release of painful feelings triggers the pain of our unreleased hurts. Once their cup spills, children lose control. Since we can't usually calm the child, it helps to focus on keeping ourselves calm. Children depend on adults to be their safety net. A child lost in a tantrum needs the adult to stay calm and keep him from hurting anyone or anything while the hurt empties out.

Crying and tantrums are not misbehaviors or manipulation; they are healing behaviors. Tantrums appear to be manipulation because the most common trigger for a tantrum is the disappointment and feeling of loss a child experiences when we say "No." The "no" is the last straw, the final drop that unleashes the hurt. Children grieve the loss they experience when we deny their request. If this "no" is the hurt that occurs when there is no more room in the cup, the cup spills.

Whenever we say no to a child, either we can expect a little crying to grieve the disappointment or we can expect a tantrum.

There is a bright side to tantrums. Releasing the pain of emotional hurt clears the way for emotional connection. Any parent who has been with a child after a full-blown tantrum has probably experienced the "rainbow after the storm." Once the child releases the pain, the child's delightful, natural nature returns. The child is usually calm, cheerful, affectionate, and cooperative.

Looking for a Limit

Have you ever heard the expression "cruising for a bruising"? Do you ever have days when it feels like children are pushing the limits and being demanding? When a child's stored hurts cup is full, the child might push for the "No" that will be the final hurt that spills the cup. The child is not cruising for a bruising. The child is looking for a limit. You do yourself and the child a service if you set a limit. Trust and know that the child will release the stored hurts and feel better when the cup is emptied.

A Reason to Cry

Making the change from interrupting the release of feelings to supporting that release is a challenge. It is also an opportunity to connect strongly with your child. The more we know about supporting the emotional healing process, the better we listen instead of interfering. It is easier to accept a child's release of feelings when we understand why a child feels hurt. It is more difficult to listen when we don't know why the child feels hurt, or we judge the hurt to be no reason to cry. There is no such thing as "no reason to cry."

Summary points on why children cry:

• If someone is crying, there is a hurt.

• Because no one knows what it feels like to be inside another person's body, we cannot make a judgment that another person has no reason to cry.

• We may not know what is causing the painful feelings, but we do know how to listen.

• It matters that we listen, not that we understand.

• When children hurt, they need to express and release their feelings to heal the hurt.

Don't Take Release of Hurts Personally

When children (and adults) hurt, they sometimes release the hurt by speaking or behaving in hurtful ways. Their release may be a verbal attack on the listener. It is not easy to listen when we feel attacked. We listen better when we remember feelings are not facts; and when we remember not to take the release of feelings personally. When a child says, "I hate you!" the child is using the most powerful word she knows to express the intensity of her feelings. The child doesn't hate you; she hates the pain she is feeling.

Acceptable Outlets for Releasing Feelings

Feelings are not right or wrong. We accept all feelings. We do not accept all behaviors. There are acceptable and unacceptable ways of expressing feelings. We allow Billy to express his angry feelings. We don't allow Billy to express his angry feelings by hitting Tommy with a truck. When Billy is angry, adrenaline floods his body. He hits, kicks, pushes, spits, bites, or throws because he doesn't know what to do with that surge of energy.

Children need adults to provide acceptable outlets for their adrenaline rather than shutting it down. We support children in healing their emotional hurts when we help them redirect their anger energy. The time to introduce acceptable outlets for anger is before anger erupts. Providing clay to pound, newspaper to rip, or a mad pillow to hit gives children acceptable ways to express their anger.

Children also need to see adults model using acceptable outlets to express anger. If an adult expresses anger by ripping newspapers, then the children will imitate that behavior. If an adult expresses anger by swearing and slamming the door, the child will too.

 In your Parenting Journal:

Write what you recall about how your parents expressed anger. Describe how you express anger. Do you ever express anger in the same ways your parents did?

A Hurt-filled Child

Sometimes children release their hurt or anger by hurting another child. Children only hurt others when they are hurting. *A hurtful child is a "hurt-filled" child.* When we punish a child for being hurtful, we hurt the already hurting child. Punishment does not take away the hurt or teach the child not to hurt others. Trying to change the hurtful behavior of an aching child by punishing her is like pulling off only the top part of a weed. If we don't get to the root, the hurtful behavior pops up elsewhere. As long as the child carries the hurt, the hurtful behavior will erupt again.

Time-out

Many children are sent to time-out when they hurt another child. Time-out is a punishment. Sending a child to time-out for hurting another child is like hitting pause on the VCR. The hurtful behavior stops only during the pause. When the child is allowed to play again, the hurtful behavior continues because the hurt is not released. Forcing a child to go to time-out doesn't work; moreover, it causes disconnection. Forced time-out is coercion. Children don't stay in time-out because they want to. They stay in time-out, if they stay, out of fear.

Conflicting Parenting Advice

Many parenting experts tell parents to use time-out to discipline. Time-out is not discipline; it is punishment. While ion Parenting

time-out is less physically hurtful than corporal punishment, it is still punishment. Time-out is emotionally hurtful and causes disconnection. Advice that undermines connection weakens the parent-child bond and is counter-productive to effective parenting.

Time-In

When I learned how we heal from emotional hurts, and that time-out teaches children to stuff their feelings, I knew I had to find another response to children. I changed time-out to time-in. A hurt-filled child needs safety. Time-in creates safety through connection.

Practicing Time-In

After attending to the child who got hurt, connect with the hurt-filled child by asking her to sit with you. Create safety by saying; "Can you tell me what is hurting you that made you hurt your friend? I know you wouldn't hurt your friend unless something was hurting you." Seeing the best in the child creates connection and safety. The child may not be able to tell you about the hurt with words. The safety of connection allows the child to release the hurt. The child releases either by crying or by raging. Once the child releases the painful feelings and heals the hurt, the hurtful behavior ceases.

Time-out Is for Adults

There is a place for time-out. Time-out is to be taken, not

given. If a child's release of painful feelings triggers an adult's stored hurt, and the adult becomes angry, the adult takes a time-out. When adults take a time-out to calm down, children learn to do the same.

Facilitating Emotional Healing by Intentionally Creating Safety

No matter how many messages we give children that it is okay to release their feelings, they get so many messages from the rest of the world that it is **not** okay, that they will still store hurts instead of releasing them. We proactively reduce temper tantrums when we intentionally create safety at the time the hurts occur.

Stored hurts not only build up to a tantrum; they block the channel for connection. Intentionally creating safety allows the child to release the painful feelings in the moment and controlling and storing hurts is reduced.

Time-in is an example of intentionally creating safety. We support the natural healing process when we refrain from interrupting the release of feelings. We facilitate the healing process when we intentionally create safety by connecting. We connect by acknowledging, validating, accepting, and listening to feelings.

Practicing Facilitating Healing by Intentionally Creating Safety

Acknowledge the feelings: "You feel really sad right now."

Validate the feelings: "It's really hard to say goodbye isn't it?"

Accept the feelings: "It's okay to cry."

Listen to the feelings: "I'll hold you and be with you while you cry."

An emotional hurt is like a splinter. Facilitating emotional healing is like taking out a splinter. When we get a splinter, the finger hurts until the splinter comes out. Taking out a splinter is not pleasant, but we don't leave splinters in because it's unpleasant to take them out. Facilitating emotional healing is not a pleasant job either, but we do it because the healing can't happen until the splinter of emotional hurt comes out. *Until the hurt comes out, the love can't get in.*

Cleaning House

You may encounter the backlog from the "black bog." A child may cry about a pet that died three years ago. The backlog of hurts in the black bog, at the bottom of the cup, surfaces when we allow the release of feelings. It feels like you have created a crying monster until the old hurts empty out. As the cup empties, the rate of release slows down, and we do not have to listen to feelings so frequently.

When We Can't Listen

We won't always be able to listen. Sometimes we reach our limit of being able to listen. When a child's release of painful feelings, triggers our unhealed hurts, we can no longer listen because our attention shifts to our stored pain. We use our control not to release our painful feelings on the child. Now is the time to take a time-out and give the child a distraction.

Distraction doesn't give a child a negative message about releasing feelings. We can say, "I need a time-out from listening. Do you need to keep crying or can you take a break from crying and get a drink of water or look at some books?" Distracting a child from completing the release only postpones it. The hurt goes back into storage and comes out at another time when triggered by another hurt.

Distraction doesn't always interrupt the release. If the child can't stop, she will continue on her own. Meantime, take a deep breath and distract yourself. A very young child will usually follow you if you try to leave the room for your time-out. You may have to sit down and disengage until either your upset subsides or the child's does.

We may not always be able to listen for as long as they need, at the time they need. We listen as often and as long as we can. When we listen, we support children's emotional health and healing, and clear the channel for connection.

What do we do with our stress and stored emotional hurts?

We learned control behaviors when we were children. As adults, we no longer have a cup to hold our accumulated hurts. We have a lake of unshed tears and unhealed hurts. In order not to feel those painful feelings, we may numb out that emotional pain with nicotine, alcohol, drugs, excessive eating, excessive shopping, excessive television viewing, and excessive working.

To be the loving parents we want to be, we need opportunities to release our old hurts and current stresses. We can't connect with children or listen to their feelings when our attention is on our pain and stress. Our connection channel becomes blocked with stress. Adults can provide stress release for each other by taking turns listening to each other. When two adults have this information, they can support each other through listening sessions.

This is how listening sessions work. Each person gets the same amount of time. Listening partners listen to each other without giving advice, trying to fix it, or asking questions. The adult being heard gets to release painful feelings from current stresses and old hurts. When the agreed upon amount of time ends, the listening partners switch roles.

Listening partners create safety for each other by agreeing to confidentiality. Each partner agrees not to repeat anything said in the listening session without asking permission. Adults who have regular opportunities to release emotional hurts and stresses, feel happier, enjoy children more, and have increased ability to listen to children's feelings.

Connecting through listening to children's feelings is a challenging and rewarding part of loving and caring for children.

Listening to children's feelings is vital to maintaining a strong bond. Once we learn to acknowledge, validate, accept, and listen to children's feelings, parenting is forever different. Responding to children's feelings with love and listening is one of the most powerful ways we connect with children.

 In your Parenting Journal

Look at your parenting goals. How will listening to your children's feelings support you in what you want to give to your children?

Look at your parenting challenges list. How will listening sessions with another adult support you in avoiding passing on hurts?

The "Connecting through listening to children's feelings" process is derived from the work of Patty Wipfler, founder of The Parents Leadership Institute in Palo Alto, California, and sixteen years of experience teaching my "Healing the Feeling Child" workshop.

This chapter on clearing the way for connection through listening to children's feelings is only the beginning of what you can learn about the value and process of listening to children and adults.

Raising Your Spirited Child by Mary Sheedy Kurcinka.

 The Explosive Child by Ross Greene

 Aletha Solter –***The Aware Baby, Tears and Tantrums, and How Young Children Flourish*** www.awareparenting.com

 Playful Parenting by Lawrence J. Cohen, Ph.D. www.playfulparenting.com

 Patty Wipfler's Parent Leadership Institute workshops, booklets, tapes, and website are rich resources for adults who want to become more skilled at listening to children and other adults. www.parentleaders.org

Chapter 4
Connecting Through Filling the Love Cup

"How we treat the child, the child will treat the world."

Human beings have a nutritional need for vitamin C and when that need is not met, we cannot survive. For example, sailors died from scurvy on long sea voyages because they didn't know about a vital missing element in their diet. In 1747, a ship's doctor, James Lind, discovered that something in citrus fruits cured scurvy. Nearly fifty years later, in 1795, when the British Royal Navy began supplementing the sailors' diet with a daily ration of lime or lemon juice, sailors stopped dying of scurvy.

Human beings also have a biological and emotional need for human connection. When that need is not met, we survive but we do not thrive. Human beings have an incredible ability to adapt to most living conditions that allow us to survive. However, we do not thrive when we have to adapt to living conditions that do not meet our biological and emotional needs.

Children today have to adapt to living conditions that do not meet their biological and emotional needs. A vital element is missing in their living conditions. The sailors were unaware that they were missing a dietary element essential to their health. As a culture we have been unaware that the essential element, key to children's wellbeing, is missing for many children in today's lifestyle.

The element missing in the sailors' living conditions was foods containing vitamin C. The missing element in our children's living conditions is also "C" – connection. Just as we have a minimum daily requirement of vitamin C to survive, we have a minimum daily requirement of human connection to thrive.

There is, and has been for decades, an abundance of well-documented research confirming that a strong parent-child connection is essential to optimal brain development. Connection, and lack of adequate connection, affects children's physical, psychological, and emotional wellbeing.

Children's need for a strong parent-child connection used to be met naturally by how we birthed and nurtured children and by our lifestyle. Over time, changes in the way we birth and nurture children, combined with today's hectic lifestyle, have compromised drastically the strength of the parent-child connection.

Parents today have busier lives, less support from extended family, and less time with their children than ever before. Between work, childcare, school, lessons, and activities, many parents and children are together for only a few waking hours a day. Even when we are with our children, we are preoccupied with daily life maintenance, the telephone, the television, the computer, and the stress of trying to do more than we have time to do.

Just keeping a roof over their heads, food on the table, and clothes on their backs (as our parents used to say) demands so much of parents that there is little time or energy left for loving connection. The strength of the parent-child bond has not been compromised by lack of love, it has been compromised by our lifestyle. While Connection Parenting won't give you more time, it will support you in spending the time you do have with your children, in ways that meet their emotional need for connection.

Children need at least one person in their life who thinks the sun rises and sets on them, someone who delights in their existence and loves them unconditionally. In today's lifestyle, having the time and attention to delight in our children is as difficult as trying to stop and smell the roses while running a marathon. However, if we knew that smelling the pleasant aroma of the roses would spur us on to win the race, we would pace ourselves to include rose- smelling time. Once we become aware of children's biological and emotional needs, we can learn to nurture them in ways that meet those needs.

Two of children's most important emotional needs are healthy self-worth and healthy self-esteem. Children's self-worth is their belief about their worthiness, what they believe about how they deserve to be treated. Their self-esteem is their belief about how capable, competent, and valued they are. Children are not born with any beliefs about themselves. Children learn what to believe about themselves from how we treat them.

Children always believe they deserve how we treat them.

If we treat children lovingly, they believe they are lovable. If we treat them badly, they believe they are bad. Children who are not treated as worthy and valuable believe there is something wrong with them. They believe "it is me" rather than there is something wrong with the way they are being treated. How we treat children determines whether they have healthy or unhealthy self-worth and self-esteem.

There are two lasting bequests we can give our children: One is roots; the other is wings. - Hodding Carter

Giving children "roots and wings"

The gift of roots is the gift of healthy self-worth. Healthy self-worth is a core belief that one's needs matter and that one is worthy of being treated with love and respect. We give children the gift of roots and a strong bond by spending enough time connecting with them to give them the message that they are worthy of love. When we treat children lovingly, they learn to love themselves and others.

The gift of wings is the gift of healthy self-esteem. Healthy self-esteem is a core belief that one is capable, competent, and valued by others. We give children the gift of wings by allowing them to do what we do and providing opportunities for them to become capable and feel valued. When we value children, they learn to value themselves and others.

The Roots of Healthy Self-worth:

Filling the Love Cup

Just as children have a cup to store their unreleased hurts, they have an emotional fuel tank or love cup. Children's love cup holds their emotional fuel. Their emotional fuel is the attention, connection, and nurturing they receive from the people they love.

Meeting children's emotional need for connection by filling their love cup is as important as meeting their physical need for food. Spending time filling a child's love cup is proactive parenting. Just as children get cranky when they get hungry, they get cranky when their love cup gets low on emotional fuel. Most difficult behaviors are either the release of emotional pain – a hurts-cup spillover or a communication signaling lack of connection - an empty love cup.

Filling the Love Cup with "High" Quality Time

In today's culture, we talk about spending quality time with children. We know that children need attention, but attention is not the same as connection. We can pay attention to children and still not connect with them emotionally. Children need **high** quality time to meet their minimum daily requirement for connection. We provide high quality time by engaging with children.

Adults consider taking children to the playground spending quality time with them. For children, *quality* is determined by "how" we spend time with them. Taking children to the playground and watching them play is quality time because we are giving them attention by watching and acknowledging their gravity-defying feats on the monkey bars. Playing tag with children at the playground is **high** quality time because we connect by engaging in the activity **with** them. We give children attention by watching and acknowledging them. We provide connection by engaging with them. Attention feels good, but connection feels better. ***Children seeking attention are requesting connection.***

> *The single most important skill parents*
> *can acquire is playing.*
>
> – *Lawrence J. Cohen author* ***Playful Parenting***

Filling the Love Cup with Play

Actively playing with children is the most powerful way we connect and fill a child's love cup. The kind of play children crave the most is the kind of play most parents do the least. This is the physically active play of chase and capture, hide and seek, piggybacks, pony rides, and the roughhouse wrestling that makes children giggle and laugh and ask for more, more, and more. This kind of play emotionally connects adults and children and strengthens the bond.

Most parents actively play with babies. We patty-cake, peek-a-boo, and bounce them on our knees. We sacrifice all dignity doing silly things to make babies laugh. However, once they are bigger and can play by themselves or with other children, we usually spend much less time actively playing with our children.

There are some adults, often, but not always, dads, who seem to excel naturally at this kind of physical play. However, few children get as much as they need of this kind of play. Whether we don't have the energy, are too distracted, too busy, or we just never learned how, because no one played actively with us, we usually aren't as playful as our children beg us to be.

Even if playing doesn't come naturally to us, we can learn how to be more playful, and communicate our love for our children in ways that strengthen our connection. Lawrence J. Cohen, author of one of my favorite parenting books, *Playful Parenting,* says, "Unlike many personality changes we might like to make, better playing skills can be pretty easily learned."

I can confirm that what he says is true. I have never been one of those adults who excelled at physical play. I didn't get much of that kind of play as a child, thus, I didn't initiate that kind of play with my children or my grandchildren. Since reading Cohen's book, to the delight of my grandchildren and their friends, I'm getting good at playing, roughhousing, and silliness.

For parents like me, for whom physically active play doesn't come naturally, learning to play is work. The exciting aspect of the work of learning to play is, the pay is priceless. The smiles, giggles, laughter, affection, and connection that bubble up from a rollicking playtime can change our whole day, even our whole relationship with a child.

Knowing first hand, the value of this kind of play, and hearing the excited reports of parents' experiences with being more playful, I now see play as one of the most important ways we connect with our children. Play is the language of children. As Cohen points out, children already know how to use play to connect, to heal their hurts, and develop confidence. Physically active play not only fills a child's need for attention; it fills the need for touch and deep connection.

Children lose confidence when they feel powerless. They disconnect either by withdrawing or by trying to control things. We help children regain their confidence when we play role reversal games that put the child in the powerful role. Nothing gives us a more accurate picture of how our children see us than playing the "pretend the child is parent and the parent is the child" game. Children delight in making us brush our teeth and forbidding us to jump on the bed. The more we beg them for what we want, the more they laugh.

Laughing together is a powerful way of connecting with each other. Children delight in silliness and often use it to try to connect when they need a refill. Instead of thwarting silliness, we can initiate it, or at least join in. We can usually turn the tide of a power struggle by getting silly instead of bossy. When children are giggling over our silliness, they are also reconnecting and getting the refill they were requesting through the power-struggle behavior.

While the *quality* of the time we spend with children cannot replace the *quantity* of time children need with us, we increase the quality of connection when we actively engage with children. Filling children's love cup with the eye contact, physical touch, laughter, and connection that occurs during play makes play the "high test" of emotional fuel.

Filling the Love Cup with One-On-One Connection Time

We spend high quality time with children when we play together on a family outing. One-on-one connection time is different from high quality time. Connection time is time spent connecting one-on-one and is essential to maintaining connection in any close relationship. Just as couples need alone-together time to maintain their connection, children need one-on-one time with the people they love.

A weekly one-on-one date provides connection time to build a strong bond. One mother shared that she turns the weekly grocery shopping into one-on-one time by rotating whose turn it is each week to help her shop and stopping for a special treat on the way home. One dad shared that he spends one-on-one time with his children by taking turns taking his children on a date to, what he calls, "go out for coffee."

How we spend one-on-one connection time with each child depends on the child's age and interests. The more time we spend with a child, the more we know the child. The more we know a child, the better we become at spending connection time in a way that fills her cup. One-on-one time may take many different forms as long as it is time spent together that is fun and fills the child's love cup with the feelings of being noticed, accepted, and loved.

Many children refer to one-on-one time as "special time." While one-on-one time is special because it makes children feel special, it is not an extra privilege to be given as a reward for *good behavior* or to be withdrawn for *unacceptable* behavior. Children need connection time as much as they need to eat and sleep.

Making the commitment to spend one-on-one connection time is an investment in your relationship with your child.

Connection Parenting Principles:

#1 We meet children's emotional needs best when we listen enough to keep their hurts cup empty and connect enough to keep their love cup full.

#2 Children who feel connected are happier, healthier, more loving, and more cooperative.

#3 Uncooperative behavior is often a communication of the unmet need for connection.

#4 The level of cooperation parents get from their children is usually equal to the level of connection children feel with their parents.

#5 Spending one-on-one time with our children does not take "extra" time.

#6 It takes the same amount of time and attention to meet children's emotional needs as it does to deal with behaviors caused by their unmet emotional needs.

#7 Either we spend time meeting children's emotional needs by filling their love cup or we will spend time dealing with behaviors caused by their unmet needs. Either way we spend the time.

Special Time

Children love it when we give their "special" time a special name. Your child's name is special. My granddaughter and I call our one-on-one special time "Maggie time." Giving connection time a name gives children a new way to request connection. Instead of communicating their need for connection through their behavior, they can "use their words."

Filling the Love Cup Every Day

Most adults have close friends and family members with whom they have a bond. No matter how long it has been since they've seen each other, they can always pick up where they left off the last time they were together. These bonds have formed over many years of sharing experiences of closeness.

Unlike adult bonds, children's bonds are still forming. It's not enough for children to know we love them. Children need to feel connected. If a young child doesn't see Grandma for six months, no matter how close and connected they became during their last visit, it usually takes some time to re-connect and re-establish trust and closeness. Children need daily doses of closeness and connection to build and maintain a secure bond.

Children are like re-chargeable batteries, and the people with whom they bond are their re-chargers. The younger they are the more often children need to connect with their parents. If we observe toddlers, we see them play, explore, and frequently return to check-in and connect with their parents for a quick recharge. As children get older, they can go longer before they need a connection re-charge but not too long.

Children use up their emotional fuel getting through the day. The more stress children experience, the more emotional fuel they use. Just as we feed children nutritious food every day, we refill their love cup with emotional fuel every day. We would never tell a child, "We don't have time to eat today but we will eat all day on Saturday."

Weekly one-on-one connection time together builds the bond; daily one-on-one time maintains the connection.

Making Time for One-On-One Connection Time

Somewhere I read that people need fifteen minutes of one-on-one, human connection, each day to feel safe. Of course, this does not mean that children need to spend "only" fifteen minutes a day with their parents. It means that, in order to feel safe, children need at least fifteen minutes a day of the time they spend with their parents to be one-on-one connection time.

While fifteen minutes a day may be the ideal, spending even ten minutes a day of one-on-one time with your child provides the consistent connection children need to maintain a strong parent-child bond.

In today's hectic lifestyle, we need to schedule one-on-one connection time with the people we live with, and love the most, if we are to meet our children's biological minimum daily requirement of connection to build and maintain a strong bond. Even ten minutes of one-on-one time a day, for each child, is a challenge to accomplish on busy days. For parents who have three children, that is a total of thirty minutes a day.

Providing one-on-one connection time with each child requires planning, communication, and flexibility.

Planning:

While one-on-one time doesn't take extra time, it does take extra effort. With everyone in the family going in different directions, weekly and daily one-on-one connection time isn't likely to happen without planning how and when we are going to have that time together.

Since every family situation is unique, there is no one way to make it happen. Some parents stagger the children's bedtimes and spend one-on-one time with each child in the evening. Some parents spend time with the older child while the younger one is napping or they spend time with the younger one before the older one gets home from school. Couples often trade off so that each child can have one-on-one with each parent. The more children you have, the more planning it requires to make sure each child gets one-on-one connection time.

Communication:

Families with more than one child and single parent families will need to enlist the support of others to make opportunities for one-on-one time with each child. Communication is vital to planning when and how we will arrange for the support to create that time. It helps to look at the month ahead, the week ahead, and sometimes even the day ahead, to find times that will work for everyone.

Flexibility:

Planning would be simple if we could plan to do one-on-one connection time with each child at a certain time each day. However, even if we plan that certain time every day, unexpected events change our plans. While it is important to make plans, we also have to be flexible about our plans. We may plan to spend special time later in the day, only to find that a child needs connection time in the morning. If we aren't able to do one-on-one time as planned, we don't give it up for the day like a missed appointment; we reschedule.

Be flexible and try to find another window of time somewhere else in the day. Create an opening for one-on-one time by having fun together on the way to or from an errand or appointment. We must plan for time together, *and* we must become masters at seizing the day, the hour, and the moment.

Rituals are moments taken solely for the purpose of connecting. – Becky Bailey Ph.D.

Filling the Love Cup with Rituals

Another way that we provide connection is through rituals. In her book, *I Love You Rituals*, Becky Bailey teaches parents to provide daily doses of closeness through creating connection rituals. We can provide connecting moments to fill the love cup by creating rituals for bedtime, wake up, mealtimes, hellos, good-byes, baths, seasonal changes, birthdays, and holidays.

You probably already do connection rituals that you have never called rituals. Singing together in the car, dancing around the dining room after dinner, and making pancakes together on Sunday morning are all rituals when we do them regularly. The more rituals we create, the more we create opportunities for connection.

By taking a few moments to notice a child, to touch a child in a loving way, or to be silly instead of serious, we create moments of closeness that fill the love cup with connection. When we say goodnight we can ask our children, "What made you feel loved today?" If we are spending moments of one-on-one connection time daily, they will be able to tell us at least one thing.

Filling children's love cup gives them the gift of healthy self-worth, which is really self-love. Self-love is vital to becoming a loving human being. Many of us grew up being taught that it was being conceited to think too highly of ourselves. We weren't taught to love ourselves. Then, we grow up and we are told that we can't possibly love anyone else until we learn to love ourselves! We teach our children to love themselves by loving them. We love them by noticing, accepting, and appreciating them, and by spending time connecting with them.

The Wings of Healthy Self-esteem

Filling children's love cup with connection meets their emotional need for healthy self-worth. To meet their emotional need for healthy self-esteem we fill their love cup with confidence. Parents do much for their children to let them know they are loved. However, knowing they are loved is not enough. Children need to feel valued. Children gain competence and confidence from what we do "with" them rather than from what we do "for" them. When children work with us they learn how to do for themselves and for others. When they can do for themselves and make a contribution to others, they feel competent and valued.

There was a time when children's contributions helped the family survive. Children's contributions to the family were valued, and children were considered assets. This is no longer true in our society. The work most parents do today does not require the help of their children. In today's society, children are considered liabilities because they hinder parents' availability to work outside the home.

Children want, need, and can do meaningful work. Though children usually cannot help their parents with their work outside the home, it is vital to children's self-esteem that we allow and encourage children to participate in the work we do at home. We reinstate children as assets to the family when we provide opportunities for them to become capable and valuable.

Children learn by doing. Learning to do new things takes time and practice. Giving children opportunities to become capable, competent and confident requires a willingness to give up perfect. It is quicker and easier to do it ourselves because we've had lots of practice. Letting young children help takes time and patience, but the more often we let children help, the sooner they become capable of making a real contribution.

Children have a similar "Catch 22" that adults have. We can't get a job if we have no experience, but we can't get experience unless we can get a job. Adults don't let children do things because they don't know how, and children don't know how unless we let them do things.

Parents assign children chores to teach them responsibility. Children resist doing their chores when chores are jobs that children are sent to do by themselves. Children want to help, but they also want to be with us and to do what we do. We get a very different response to doing chores when we say, "Let's do this job together."

Children love to help us make dinner, wash the car, plant the garden, and rake the leaves. The chores that adults view as work, children view as play. Adults are product-oriented. We want to get the job done and get the result. Young children are process-oriented. For them, process is everything. They are thrilled to break the eggs and stir the batter, and may not even care about eating the muffin once it is baked.

We can turn a chore into connection time by including children in the process. When children need connection and we need to make dinner, we meet everyone's needs by letting them help make dinner. Letting children help is a double win-win. We get dinner made and provide connection time all at once. Children get the connection they need and an opportunity to build confidence by becoming competent. Working together builds healthy self-worth and self-esteem!

Allowing children to work with us is only one of the ways we fill children's love cup with confidence and build healthy self-esteem. Children are born with gifts. Some children are naturally artistic, musical, athletic, or mechanical. Some children love animals, books, bugs, or ballet. Children feel valued when we respond to their interests and gifts with encouragement and provide opportunities for them to follow their interests and develop their gifts. Filling children's love cup with confidence gives them the wings of healthy self-esteem.

A child is not born a Gandhi or a Hitler. Children are born with temperament, needs, gifts, and potential. How those unfold depends on how we treat them. Both nature and nurture determine who children become.

In his book, *Instead of Education,* John Holt compared human beings to bonsai trees. The seedling you bonsai, by clipping its roots, wiring its branches, and depriving it of what it needs in the early stage of its development, becomes a dwarfed miniature of the potential within that seedling. If that same seedling is given what it needs, it grows straight and tall. Human beings can also become dwarfed miniatures of their innate potential when they are deprived of what they need in the early stages of their development.

What people become under one set of circumstances does not tell us very much about what they might have become under another. – John Holt

The childhood experiences of Gandhi, the man of peace, and Hitler, the man of war, were as opposite as the adults they became. Little Mohandas Gandhi had a loving, strong bond with both his parents. Little Adolf Hitler was severely abused. They had completely different childhood experiences and role models. Gandhi brought to the world the lessons of peace and love he experienced and learned in his family. Hitler brought to the world the violence and humiliation he experienced and learned in his family. Who might little Adolf have become if he had grown up in the Gandhi family?

Resiliency research shows that children who overcome an abusive and/or neglectful childhood and become adults who do well in their lives had at least one person who connected with them. If those children had the potential to succeed in spite of abuse, and unmet needs, whom would they be if nurtured and loved?

Let's raise children who won't have to recover from their childhood.

Children who have been loved and encouraged have healthier self-worth and self-esteem than those who have not been well treated. How well children cope with change, stress, loss, and uncertainty depends on:

• How securely bonded they are

• What we teach them to believe about themselves

• How connected they feel

- How much safety they are given to release and heal their emotional hurts

- Their innate temperament and sensitivities

We nurture our children's resilience when we focus on their strengths, spend enough time with them to stay connected, and create safe spaces for them to work through their fears and feelings. Children with healthy self-worth and self-esteem are emotionally strong. We can't protect our children from the inevitable stresses and losses that are part of living, but we can help them build their boat strong enough to weather the storms of life.

> Until we can give our children a better world,
> we'll have to give our world more
> resilient children.

We have the opportunity and responsibility to nurture and protect our children's human potential. When we give children the gifts of feeling loved and valued, they can use their roots and wings to give their gifts to the world.

Filling the Love Cup

Tell your listening partner, or write in your parenting journal, one experience when an adult spent one-on-one time with you. How old were you? What were the circumstances? How did you feel? Tell your listening partner, or write in your parenting journal, something you felt valued for in your family.

In your Parenting Journal:

Write a list of ways to spend one-on-one connection time with each of your children.

Write a list of the rituals you already have and ideas for new ones.

Write a list of home tasks that you can do with your children.

Write a list of ways to notice, encourage, and support your children's interests and gifts.

 Your Child's Self-esteem by Dorothy Corkhill Briggs

Playful Parenting by Lawrence J. Cohen

I Love You Rituals by Becky Bailey

 *Nurture Your Child's Gift – Inspired Parenting* by Caron B. Goode

Chapter 5
Connecting through Communication
that Builds Relationship

"Please talk to me like I'm someone you love." - *A parent*

Every word we say to children affects their self-worth and self-esteem. Our words either encourage children or discourage them. How we talk and how we listen determines whether communication leads to connection and cooperation or disconnection and conflict.

Children's motivation to cooperate comes from feeling connected. Speaking respectfully and listening with love builds connection. When children feel connected to us we have influence. Speaking to children in disrespectful, unloving ways breaks connection. When we break connection, we lose influence. Without influence, we resort to coercion.

When connection is weak or broken and children are not cooperating, we feel frustrated or angry. We say the same things to children that we heard as children. We don't intend to criticize, blame, shame, threaten, or yell; but sometimes we do.

In his book, **Predictive Parenting,** Shad Helmstetter says our brains operate like tape recorders attached to computers. As children, we record and file every word we hear. Our files become the programming that runs our behavior. As adults, when our buttons get pushed, our old "tapes" automatically play, and we act from our early programming.

When children are fighting and we intervene, the first words we hear are "he/she started it." How often, when we have conflicts with our children, are we the ones who "started it" by speaking in a disrespectful way or by not listening with love.

Speaking disrespectfully breaks communication by shutting down children's listening. Being criticized, blamed, shamed, threatened, or yelled at feels like an attack. When we feel attacked, we disconnect and defend by fighting (resisting) or fleeing (ignoring). When children are defending, they have no attention or motivation for listening.

It is our responsibility to communicate in a way that allows children to listen.

Children's words don't always express what they need or feel. When we don't understand or respond to children's expression of their needs, children react in one of two ways:

They express their needs more loudly

They suppress their needs by withdrawing

We maintain connection with children when we listen for the needs and feelings behind their words.

Listening with love is listening with empathy and compassion

We listen with love to hear the needs and feelings behind children's words. Listening with love means putting our needs and feelings on hold so we can focus on the child. Instead of focusing on how the child's behavior is making you feel, you focus on how the child feels.

Listening with love examples:

"When I hear you say (or see you do) hurtful things, that tells me something is hurting you. Can you tell me about what is hurting you?"

"It sounds like you feel..." (angry, sad, disappointed, frustrated, embarrassed)

The way we talk and listen to children comes from the old programming we received as children or from new communication skills we acquire as adults.

Communicating respectfully does not mean we are never supposed to feel or express frustration or anger. It means learning to express our upset feelings in a respectful way.

We can:

• Replace our programming with new communication skills

• Express our needs and feelings in a respectful way

• Listen with love to maintain connection

• Provide children with a model of communication that builds relationship

Replacing Old Tapes with New Communications Skills

Remember: No beating ourselves up for what we didn't know OR our programming!

Saying, "Don't"

If we heard "don't" many times a day as children, we have "don't" tapes. "Don't jump on the bed. Don't hit your sister. Don't touch the stove." We are programmed to tell children what we don't want them to do, which is counterproductive to cooperation and connection.

Telling children what we don't want them to do doesn't teach them what we *want* them to do. Children cooperate more readily when we tell them what we expect. Giving information gives them the opportunity to tell themselves what to do.

Children's brains record every word we say to them. Every time we say, "Don't," children's brains record what we don't want them to do. The word don't gets their attention, but what they record is, "Jump on the bed. Hit your sister. Touch the stove."

"Don't" feels like an order and a criticism. Orders undermine children's self-worth by making them feel that their needs and feelings don't matter. Criticism erodes children's self-esteem by making them feel incapable. Orders and criticisms break connection and invite power struggles.

New Skills:

We maintain connection and reduce power struggles by respectfully telling children what we do want them to do.

Example:

Instead of "Don't hit your sister."

Give information: "Hitting hurts. You may not hit your sister."

State your feelings: "I feel upset when I see someone I love hurting someone I love."

State your need: "I need all of us to feel safe."

Listen with love: "I know you must be upset too because the only time you are hurtful to others is when something is hurting you. I'm willing to listen to your feelings."

Make a request: "Are you willing to work together to find a safe way to tell your sister how you feel?"

If the child says no, we need to do more listening. The child will be able to reconnect when all the hurt is released.

Parents in my classes are amazed when they realize how often they say "don't" and how challenging it is to stop saying don't. We cannot think clearly when our buttons have been pushed. When a child is doing something that is upsetting to us it is quicker and easier to say, "Don't do that" than to think of what we do want the child to do.

Sometimes we must protect children from their lack of information, experience, or control. When you must respond quickly, try using another word. "Stop! "Danger!" "Hot!" "Sharp!"

We may never eliminate saying, "don't," but we can reduce our use of it. When you catch yourself saying, "Don't," follow it by telling children what you do want them to do.

Yelling

Sometimes, even the most loving parents, yell at their children. Some parents yell because they were programmed to yell by being yelled at frequently as children. Others yell only when they get really frustrated or angry. Yelling hurts children's feelings, self-worth, and self-esteem, and it instantly breaks connection.

Yelling frightens children. Being yelled at is an attack and it triggers the fight or flight response. Some children defend by fighting - yelling back at us. Some children defend by fleeing - trying to escape either physically or emotionally.

Unless we are yelling, "Dinner is ready," yelling is either intentional intimidation to frighten a child into doing what the adult wants or the unintentional release of frustration or anger.

Children learn to communicate by imitating the way we communicate. Intentionally yelling at children to get them to do what we want is bullying. It teaches children to yell at people to get them to do what they want. Unintentionally yelling at children is the loss of control. It teaches children that yelling at people is an acceptable way of dealing with frustration.

While yelling is challenging programming to change, there is a simple way to interrupt yelling and reduce the emotional damage yelling causes.

New Skills:

Tell your children that you are working on not yelling and ask for their help. Give your children permission to interrupt your yelling. Tell them they can remind you to stop yelling by covering their ears as a non-verbal reminder or by saying either, "You are yelling at me and it hurts my feelings," or "Please talk to me like I'm someone you love." Respond to the reminder with rewind, repair, and replay.

Example:

Rewind: "Thank you for reminding me, I forgot or I got frustrated."

Repair: "I'm sorry; you didn't deserve to be yelled at. What you did was not okay but yelling at you is not okay either."

Replay: "Let's start over. I feel frustrated because I need…"

Giving children permission to remind us not to yell:

- Empowers children to defend themselves from yelling without having to fight or flee

- Protects their self-worth by letting them know they don't deserve to be yelled at

- Builds connection by showing regard for their needs and feelings

Giving Orders

If we grew up being ordered instead of asked, we have "giving orders" tapes. Giving orders is disrespectful. It breaks connection by communicating disregard for a child's needs and feelings.

New Skills:

We maintain connection and foster cooperation when we give invitations – "Let's", and by using transition information phrases – "It's time to" – "as soon as" – "when we finish…".

Example:

Instead of "Go brush your teeth."

Invitation: "Let's go brush our teeth."

Transition information: "It's time for teeth brushing." "As soon as teeth brushing is done, it will be story time." "When we finish our snack it will be time for teeth brushing."

When invitations and transition information don't result in cooperation, there is a disconnection or a non-relationship cause for the behavior.

Warnings

We are programmed to remind children to be safe by telling them to be careful. Being careful is different in every situation. Saying "Be careful" is like saying "Don't. It doesn't teach them how to be careful. By the time children are older they have heard be careful so many times they resent the implication that they don't know what to do. They respond to the reminder with "I know, I know! I'm not stupid."

New Skills

We keep children safer by giving information than by giving warnings. Young children need to learn how to be careful.

Example: "Hold onto the railing. Take small, slow steps. Use both hands"

As children get older and we have already taught them how to be safe, instead of saying, "Be careful," we ask them to tell us how they are going to be safe.

Example:

"Tell me how you will stay safe riding your bike to the store."

Asking older children to tell us how they will stay safe is a win-win. When we ask children to tell us how they will be safe they feel less annoyed than when we say, "Be careful." We still meet our need to remind them to be safe because, by them telling us how they will be safe, they remind themselves.

Other Communication Programming that Breaks Connection:

Lecturing, being sarcastic, accusing, blaming, shaming, criticizing, name-calling, and teasing

The above communication styles not only break connection, they also damage self-esteem and self worth. We interrupt those connection-breaking programs the same way we interrupt yelling.

Ask children to help you stop speaking in those ways by giving them permission to remind you to stop, by covering their ears, or by saying, "Your words are hurting my feelings or please talk to me like I'm someone you love." Respond to the child's reminder with rewind, repair, and replay.

Example:

Rewind: "Thank you for reminding me. I got upset and forgot."

Repair: "I'm sorry. I didn't mean to hurt your feelings. You don't deserve to be spoken to that way."

Replay: "I don't like what you did, but I always love you. I want to start over."

The most effective way I know, of speaking respectfully and to listen with love, I learned from the Nonviolent Communication SM (NVC) Process, developed and taught by Marshall Rosenberg, Ph.D.

The speaking process uses "I" messages to describe what you are experiencing.

Observation: "When I see…"

State what you see without interpretation or judgment.

Feelings: "I feel…"

State your feelings rather than your thoughts.

Needs: "…because I need."

State your need or a value rather than a preference or a specific action.

Requests: "Would you be willing to…?"

State a concrete action you would request to be taken rather than make a demand.

Example of using this process to maintain connection:

Observation: "When I see toys all over the living room…"

Feelings: "I feel frustrated…"

Needs: "Because I need help keeping the house in order."

Request: "Would you be willing to pick them up now?"

If the answer is no, there is disconnection (or another behavioral cause) because when children feel connected they care about our needs and feelings. We reconnect through listening with love.

Speaking in "I" statements allows the listener to listen instead of defend.

The listening process uses "You" messages to describe your understanding of the other person's experience.

Observation: "When you see …"

Feelings: "You feel …"

Needs: "Because you need…"

Requests: "You would like…?"

Example of using this process to maintain connection by listening with love:

Observation: "When you hear me asking you to pick up your toys again."

Feelings: "You feel annoyed?"

Needs: "Because you need to do something, else right now?"

Requests: "Would you like me to ask you when you will be ready to pick up the toys?"

Listening through "You" statements allows you to check your understanding of the other person's experience. It allows the other person to feel understood or to correct your understanding.

Learning to speak and listen in these loving, respectful ways takes time, effort, and practice. The extra time we spend now, learning to maintain connection by communicating respectfully, we save later in the extra time we won't spend reconnecting with rewind, repair, and replay.

In carpentry, there is a guideline for saving time and work: Measure twice, cut once. In Connection Parenting, the guideline for saving time and work is: Think twice, speak once. It is less work and takes less time to stop and think before we speak. Otherwise, you do the reconnection work every time you break connection by speaking, without stopping to think about how to communicate respectfully.

Communication Skills that Build Connection, Self-worth, and Self-esteem

Listening with your eyes as well as with your heart:

Imagine how it feels to be three and always talking to an adult's knees. When speaking to children it is respectful to position your body to be on eye level with the child. Eye contact let's children know we are listening.

Saying yes instead of no as often as possible:

Other than "Mama" or "Dada," most children's first word is "No" because they hear it the most. Children grow up hearing far more of what they can't do than what they can do. Children with healthy self-esteem have a "can do" attitude. We support a can do attitude toward life when we support children in looking for what they can do.

When children are doing something we don't want them to do, we can tell them what they can do. If children make a request that we can't honor at the moment, if we stop and think before we say no, we can tell them when they *can* do, what they can't do now.

Example:

Instead of saying no when toddlers reach for the forbidden,

pick up something they can touch and say, "Here, this is for you."

Instead of saying no when a child asks for a cookie, say, "Yes, you may have one after dinner."

Instead of saying no when a teenager asks to attend a party, say "Yes, if you can satisfy all my concerns."

Giving choices:

There are many circumstances in children's lives over which they have no control or choice. Children need some power and control over their life. We empower children and avoid power struggles when we offer choices. Choices need to be in keeping with the child's age and the information and experience they have to make choices.

Examples:

"Do you want the red cup or the blue one? Do you want eggs or cereal? Do you want to go to the playground or have a friend over today?"

Asking children what they want for dinner or what they want to do is frustrating to them. That is too many choices.

Even when there is no choice about what to do, there is usually a choice about *how* to do it.

Example:

"The doctor says you need to take this medicine to get well. Not taking the medicine is not a choice. Do you want to take it in a spoon or in some applesauce? Do you want to take it now or in five minutes? Do you want to take it in the kitchen or in the bathroom?"

In these situations, the more choices we offer, the less powerless a child feels.

If choices don't result in cooperation we need to keep stating the necessary action and keep listening to the feelings until we reach connection.

There are situations over which there is no choice.

Example:

"You may not play in the street. Playing in the street in dangerous. It's my job to keep you safe. Do you want play in the yard or in the house?"

If children refuse to choose, we need to continue to set the limit and listen to their feelings. Once they have emptied out their upset, they can think well again and make a choice.

Telling children what you need instead of telling them what they need

Some adults avoid giving orders by telling children, "You need to…"

The truth is the adult needs the child to… It is more accurate and more respectful to say, "I need you to get your shoes on so we can go."

Eliminating saying "Okay" when we are not offering a choice

Some adults try to soften orders or make sure the child heard the order by following the order with saying, "Okay?" Children are completely literal about language. Children hear the question "Okay?" as a choice and feel confused if we get upset if they say no.

Describing behavior instead of judging by criticizing or praising

Most of us grew up hearing "good girl or boy" or "bad girl or boy" depending on whether our behavior pleased or displeased adults. Judging children as bad or good sends the message that they are worthy of love only when they please us. Children need to know that they are always worthy of love, even when they make mistakes, lose control, or don't please us.

When we criticize or show our disapproval of children's behavior by saying "bad boy" or "bad girl," children hear and believe that they are bad instead of that their behavior was unacceptable. Telling children they are bad, doesn't teach them how to behave in a better way or motivate them to want to.

Saying, "Good boy" or "Good girl" is also a judgment of the child rather than the child's accomplishment. Even though praise communicates approval, approval is judgment. Children need appreciation and encouragement rather than praise and approval. Approval is not appreciation or encouragement.

The old theory about human behavior told us that praising children builds self-esteem. In addition, old theory said that if we use positive reinforcement, by praising their "good" behavior, our approval would encourage them to repeat that behavior. New research shows that praise and approval does not build self-worth and self-esteem or motivate children to do better. Children need appreciation and encouragement.

Children have a great need for connection, attention, appreciation, acceptance, and encouragement to feel good about themselves. If adults don't have influence with children through connection, they resort to threats or positive reinforcement to control children's behavior. Positive reinforcement sounds nicer than threats but both are manipulation. Threats manipulate children into complying out of their fear of punishment. Positive reinforcement manipulates children into doing what we want by taking advantage of their need for our love and acceptance.

Saying, "It makes me so happy when you share," sounds like encouragement to be generous, but it is actually manipulation. Children become motivated to share, not out of wanting to give to the other child, but out of their need for attention and approval from the adult. Praise teaches children to feel good about themselves only when they please others.

Controlling children's behavior through manipulation when they are young backfires when they are older. If children only feel good about themselves when they please others, they are more vulnerable to peer pressure. When pleasing their friends is more important to them than feeling pleased with themselves, they will choose to please their friends.

Other than attempts at positive reinforcement, praise is intended to show love and appreciation. Saying "Good girl" or "Good boy, "isn't bad, but it isn't encouragement. We can do better than that for our children.

We encourage children to feel pleased with themselves by appreciating them instead of evaluating them. We show appreciation by noticing them and describing what they are doing or have done. When your programming wants to encourage by saying, "Good boy' or "Good girl," encourage by noticing, appreciating, and describing instead.

Examples of encouraging by noticing, appreciating, and describing:

We say, "You picked up your toys. Thank you for the help!"

Child hears: I am helpful.

We say, "You left your muddy boots outside. Thank you for remembering."

Child hears: I have a good memory.

We say, "You made it to the potty, you did it!"

Child hears: I'm big. I'm capable.

We say, "You swam all the way across the pool!"

Child hears: I'm a good swimmer.

We say, "You put every piece of silverware in its own place. Thank you for organizing them."

Child hears: I'm organized.

We say, "You picked some flowers for me. Thank you for your thoughtfulness."

Child hears: I am thoughtful.

We say, "You put gas in the car before you brought it back. Thanks for taking responsibility for that."

Teen hears: I am responsible.

When we notice, describe, and appreciate what children do, they feel pleased with themselves.

Our saying "Good" is as challenging to change as our saying "Don't." While we are practicing becoming more fluent in noticing, appreciating, and describing, if "Good" is already out of your mouth before you can catch it say, "Good for you!" **then** notice, describe and appreciate.

Interrupting our old "tapes," and learning respectful speaking and listening skills are essential to parenting through connection instead of coercion. Learning new communication skills is the simple, though not easy, part. The hard part is overriding our old programming when our buttons get pushed. It is challenging not to fall back into disrespectful ways of speaking and listening that cause disconnection. That's why we need rewind, repair, and replay.

The way we talk to children will be the way they talk to us and to others. More importantly, it will be the way they talk to themselves.

Practicing Connection Communication

 In your Parenting Journal:

List the daily conflicts you have with your children. Then ask yourself, at those times of conflict when my children resist or ignore, am I either "playing my tapes" (speaking without thinking) or not listening with love?

Once we are aware of our part in creating conflict, we can override our old programming and use new communication skills to change the way we speak and listen.

As we change our behavior, children change their behavior.

 Raising Our Children Raising Ourselves
by Naomi Aldort

 Parenting From Your Heart—A presentation of Nonviolent Communication ideas and their use
by Inbal Kashtan

 How to Talk So Kids Will Listen and Listen So Kids Will Talk by Adele Faber and Elaine Mazlish

 Predictive Parenting by Shad Helmstetter

Chapter 6
Connecting through the Discipline of Decoding Children's Behavior

We can't teach children to behave better by making them feel worse.
When children feel better, they behave better.

As new parents we hear, "Enjoy your children while they are little." Yet, how much time do we spend enjoying our children? Many parents spend much of the day struggling with their children. How has this come to be? What makes parenting today more often a struggle than a joy?

Many people say, "Kids today are different, I would never have behaved that way as a child." Parents today are confronted with child behaviors that their grandparents didn't experience in raising their children. When our children's behavior drives us crazy, we need to look at our behavior:

- How much connection time have we spent with our children?
- How busy are we?
- How stressed are we?

When we are enjoying our children, we are spending time connecting with them. We aren't rushing them from one place to another. We aren't anxious, stretched too thin, and circling in busyness.

Children's behavior is different today because childhood is different today. Parents' lives are busier and more stressful than our grandparents' lives. We do more, go to more places, and expect children to keep the same pace. Children now go to day care, preschool, school, athletic games, lessons, and appointments. They often spend as much time, if not more, getting to and from these activities, as they do participating in the activity.

Children need connection time with their parents, time for unstructured play, and time to "just be." Kids don't get much of that today. Children are frequently in transition from one place to another. Most children today spend less time in their home, with their family, than children ever have.

Parents tell me that transitions are the times of the most conflict with their children. Getting them out the door in the morning and into bed at night is often a struggle. It seems that what we enjoy about children also drives us crazy about them. Children live in the **now**. Their attention is completely on what they need, feel, or are doing, **right now.**

We are not in the **now** when we are rushing to "get out the door" or trying to get them into bed. We are thinking about where we are going next and what we have to do next. We are focused on our agenda.

When children need time to connect with us, or they need time to "just be," they know that getting out the door, or going to bed means those needs won't get met. To children, transition often means sacrificing their needs to meet our needs and they naturally resist. When children resist our agenda, we see their behaviors as problems.

The reason parents, caregivers, and teachers most often state for attending my parenting workshops is that they want better tools for dealing with children's problem behaviors.

Natural logic forbids belief in the evolution of a species with the characteristic of driving its parents to distraction by the millions.
*~ Jean Leidloff author of **The Continuum Concept***

As our lifestyle and our way of birthing and nurturing children changed, the connection between parents and children began to erode. This loss of connection affected children's behavior. Children act out their unmet need for connection through behaviors that push our buttons.

It is hard to remember to use loving, respectful communication when children's behavior pushes our buttons.

What problem behaviors push your buttons?

In your Parenting Journal:

Make a list of children's behaviors that push your buttons.

In my workshops, participants create a group list of "button pushing" behaviors. Some behaviors that frequent their list:

Temper tantrums – whining – not listening – hitting – talking back – not cooperating – teasing – bullying – refusing to share – fighting with siblings – refusing to get dressed – refusing to brush their teeth – arguing – calling names – hurting others

Why are children behaving in these ways?

Children want to do well. Children want, need, and deserve to feel accepted, liked, loved, valued, and appreciated by their parents, family, friends, caregivers, teachers, classmates, and community. My experience of children is that when children's needs are met and nothing is hurting, they are happy, and their behavior is not a problem. When they are not doing well, their acting out behavior is a request for our help.

Human beings communicate in many ways. Besides using words, we communicate with our eyes, facial expressions, gestures, body language, and behavior. Because adults most often communicate verbally, we tell children, "use your words." Even when children have language, they cannot always identify and articulate their needs. When children cannot use their words, they communicate their needs by acting them out with their behavior, thus "acting out" behavior.

*...all our behavior is our constant attempt to reduce
the difference between what we want
(the pictures in our head) and what we have
(the way we see situations in the world)*

– *William Glasser, M.D. author* **Control Theory – A New
Explanation of How We Control Our Lives**

Behavior as a communication of need

Behavior is need-driven. We do what we do to get our needs met. Children depend on adults to meet their physical and emotional needs. When children have an unmet need, they feel discomfort. Because they cannot meet their own need, they must get our attention and communicate their needs, so we can help them.

Babies cry because they are in pain or to attract our attention to their needs. Parents of infants learn the difference between a cry of need and a cry of pain. However, babies give subtle cues that they have a need before they cry, such as squirming and wriggling. They cry when the need becomes painful.

When we have a strong connection with children, we are more likely to notice their early, subtle cues of need, before need escalates to pain. The less connected we are, the less likely we will notice children's cues. If we don't respond to children's cues, they **have to** become more emphatic in communicating their needs to attract our attention.

For example, a baby starts squirming and rooting when he feels the discomfort of hunger. If the mother is holding her baby, she notices the squirming and responds to the baby's communication of hunger. If the baby is alone in a crib and the mother cannot see and respond to the visual cues of the baby's need, the discomfort escalates to the pain of hunger. The baby cries from the pain and to attract mother's attention to his need.

A baby's cry is a communication designed to bother us and move us to action to meet the baby's needs. In the same light, children's needy behaviors, by design, are supposed to bother us, and move us to action to meet the child's needs.

Escalation from need to pain happens, even when children have language, if the parents do not respond to the early communications.

For example, a child very pleasantly says, "Mom, I'm hungry, when are we having lunch?" Mom is busy writing and says, " I'll just finish this paragraph and then I'll make us some lunch." Mom gets caught up in her creativity and doesn't leave her work to make lunch. The child comes back ten minutes later and finds no lunch ready and mom still at the computer. The child communicates her need more emphatically by screaming, "I'm hungry! You said you would make lunch, and you are still at the computer!"

Now the child has Mom's attention. Mom reluctantly leaves the computer, starts making the lunch, and the phone rings. The child comes into the kitchen, sees Mom on the phone, and melts down in a temper tantrum. Mom has to hang up the phone, embarrassed because she can't hear over the tantrum. Mom, frustrated by her unmet needs and the child's behavior, now has to deal with the temper tantrum.

Is the child having a tantrum because she is a "bad" child? No. Is the mom intentionally ignoring her child's needs and being a "bad" mother? No.

They were both just trying to get their needs met.

Power Struggles

Children need love most when they appear to deserve it least.

Children resort to communicating through unloving, uncooperative behaviors when they have unmet needs. Those behaviors trigger our old hurts of feeling unnoticed, unaccepted, unappreciated, or unloved. When children's behaviors push our buttons, we lock into an emotional power struggle with the child. Each of us is struggling to be the one to get our needs met.

A power struggle is two people trying to get their needs met without connection.

In his Nonviolent Communication[SM] work, Marshall B. Rosenberg, Ph.D., uses the terms "power-over" and "power-

with." His terms accurately describe the difference between disconnection and connection. A strong connection between two
people means they have influence or power "with" each other
because each has a high regard for the needs and feelings of the
other.

When there is a weak connection or disconnection between
two people, there is no high regard for each other's needs and
feelings. Without that high regard, we have no influence or
power "with" the other person. Without influence, we resort to
power "over" the other person to get what we need.

> *When you got nothing, you got nothing to lose.*
> *- Bob Dylan*

Connection means we trust that others will help us get what we
need. Trust translates into cooperation, and people work
together so they both get what they need. Without connection,
we are alone. We cannot depend on anyone else to help us get
what we need. We have to meet our needs without regard for
anyone else's needs. No trust translates into conflict.

Decoding behavior means looking for the intention behind the action.

To maintain connection by honoring children's needs and feelings, we learn to decode the language of behavior.

We already have experience in decoding behavior, especially if we have a dog. When a dog goes to the door, we decode that behavior, and let the dog out. If we do not understand what the dog's behavior means, and we don't let the dog out, the dog finally resorts to going on the floor instead of outdoors. Not understanding the dog's communication of need did not take away the dog's need.

The dog's unacceptable behavior was unmet need behavior, not bad dog behavior. When children are "acting out" to communicate a need, it is not bad child behavior. Rather it is often an unmet need behavior.

When we change our thinking about behavior, we change our language, too. Acting out behavior, misbehavior, or naughty behavior is often "needy" behavior. It is our job as adults to meet children's needs and teach them acceptable ways of communicating their need, until they are old enough to meet their own needs.

It is also our job to teach children acceptable behavior. Most adults were programmed to teach children acceptable behavior through punishing them for their unacceptable behavior. The approach that adults use to teach acceptable behavior depends on either our old programming or new information and skills.

Corporal Punishment as Discipline

Most of our parents believed that as long as hitting did no permanent physical damage, then physical punishment would "teach us a lesson." Hitting children has been accepted as a form of discipline in our society for so long that some parents cannot imagine that it is possible to discipline children without hitting them. It is not only is possible to teach children acceptable behavior without hitting them, it is impossible to teach children acceptable behavior by hitting them.

Parents *intend* to teach their children to be courteous, respectful, responsible, kind, and loving. Children learn from what we model. Hitting is not courteous, respectful, responsible, kind, or loving. Hitting is violence. When we model violence, we teach violence. The only "lessons" hitting can teach children are to hit and to fear and distrust those who hit them.

It is not nice to hit people; children are people.

Dr. Daniel F. Whiteside, former Assistant Surgeon General, reported, "Corporal punishment of children actually interferes with the process of learning and with their optimal development as socially responsible adults. We feel that it is important for public health workers, teachers, and others concerned for the emotional and physical health of children and youth to support the adoption of alternative methods for the achievement of self-control and responsible behavior in children and adolescents."

Hitting children **hurts their** bodies, hearts, and minds. Instead of sending the **message** that their behavior was bad, being hit causes children to believe that they are bad. Research shows that hitting children diminishes their self-esteem. There is even evidence from a British study that children who are hit may be less able to learn because physical punishments reduce children's IQ.

Despite all the research, which shows that hitting children fails to teach them acceptable behavior and damages them emotionally, intellectually, and physically, many children are still being hit in the name of discipline.

When I ask parents why they hit children to "discipline" them, I found three common answers.

• "I was hit when I was a kid, and it didn't hurt me any. It's the only way to make kids mind."

• "Until now, I didn't know there was anything wrong with hitting my kids. My parents hit me when I was bad, and I just thought that's how you discipline your kids."

• "I know it's not good to hit my kids, but sometimes I get angry and frustrated and I don't know what else to do."

Not all adults who were hit as children grow up to be hitters. However, most adults who hit, were hit or witnessed hitting when they were children. Adults who were hit as children say that they remember being hit, but they don't remember why. This is more evidence that hitting fails as a form of discipline.

Being hit activates the fight or flight response in human beings.

When someone hits us, our rational thinking shuts down. All we can think about is protecting ourselves by hitting back or running away. If we cannot think about *why,* or even which behavior was wrong, neither can we learn the right thing to do. We cannot teach children acceptable behavior by hitting them. Spanking is a euphemism for violence.

- When a big kid hits a little kid, we call it bullying.
- When an adult hits a child, we call it spanking.
- When an adult hits another adult, we call it assault.
- When the adults in a family hit each other we call it battering or domestic violence.

Why then, when the adults hit the children in the family, do we call it discipline? No matter what name we give it, a swat, a slap, a tap, or a spanking, corporal punishment is not discipline; it is violence.

Hitting breaks connection and trust.

Non-corporal Punishment as Discipline

Many adults who refrain from using corporal punishment use the punishments of loss of privileges, being grounded, timeout, and threats as discipline. The theory behind the use of punishment as discipline is that, if the punishment is painful or unpleasant enough, it will "teach" the child acceptable behavior by making the child fear future punishment for repeating the unacceptable behavior.

Punishing children does not teach them the intended lesson of acceptable behavior. Punishment teaches children to be sneaky, to lie, and to avoid being caught. The reality of punishment is that it is about controlling children's behavior through the use of fear. When we punish children, we model bullying. By our example, we teach children to get what they need by controlling other people through the use of fear.

We have only to look at the rate of repeat offenders in prison to see that punishment does not work to deter people from repeating unacceptable behavior. Punishment causes children to think more about the wrong that was done to them than the wrong they did. Punishment undermines children's natural desire to behave in ways that bring them love and acceptance. Using any kind of punishment as discipline breaks connection and trust.

True Parental Discipline

Most of the time, when people say discipline they mean punishment. Although we use the words punishment and discipline interchangeably, as if they have the same meaning, they are different. Punishment is defined in the dictionary as "arbitrary harsh treatment for wrong-doing." True parental discipline means teaching or training children to do what is right. Punishment is not discipline because it does not teach children to do what is right.

Making Restitution:

When you do something wrong, you can choose to make it right.

We teach children to do what is right by modeling acceptable behavior and by teaching them about making restitution. Children need to know that they can choose to make it right when they have behaved in unacceptable ways.

When our behavior as a parent is not what we want it to be, and we use the reconnection tool of rewind, repair, and replay, we model making it right through restitution. We teach children acceptable behavior by teaching them how to make it right.

- When children spill their milk, we teach them how to clean up a spill.

- When a child breaks a window, we teach him that he can choose to take responsibility for repairing or replacing it.

- When a child hurts someone's feelings, we teach her that she can choose to apologize.

Punishment gives children the message:

You did wrong and now you must suffer because you are bad.

Restitution gives children the message:

You did wrong, and now you can choose to make it right.

Punishing children teaches them to believe that they are bad. Making restitution teaches children to believe in their ability to make it right.

In the introduction to her book, *It's All About WE: Rethinking Discipline Using Restitution,* Diane Gossen describes Restitution as "*...a genuine paradigm shift from external discipline, which coerces and alienates youth to internal discipline, which strengthens and embraces youth.*"

If the only reason children have for not doing something wrong is the fear of being punished, what guidelines will they have for behavior when no one is there to punish them? The goal of true parental discipline is not to control children's behavior by hurting them when their behavior is unacceptable but rather to teach children to do what is right. We cannot control anyone's behavior but our own. True parental discipline leads children to self-discipline.

In spite of the fact that punishment doesn't teach children to do what is right, many adults still punish children for unacceptable behavior. Though punishment may stop a challenging behavior temporarily, if the behavior is a communication of an unmet need, some form of needy behavior will persist.

We cannot punish people into not having needs.

For example, I have a physical need to eat to survive. If I had no food and no legal way to get food, I would steal food rather than die. I would steal food even though I know that stealing is wrong and that I would be punished if I got caught.

If I am caught stealing food and punished, will punishing me for stealing food teach me not to be hungry? No. If I were in the same position again, with no other way to get food, I would repeat the behavior of stealing food, even though I know punishment is the consequence.

You cannot teach me to not have my physical need for food. Just as punishing me for stealing food cannot teach me to not be hungry, punishing children for needy behavior cannot teach them not to have their emotional needs of attention and connection.

When we don't meet children's emotional needs, they are compelled by their dependency to communicate their needs. When children communicate their unmet needs through their behavior and we react by punishing their behavior, we are trying to cure the symptom instead of the cause.

Though we may stop needy behavior temporarily by threatening punishment or bribing with a reward, if the need still exists, some form of acting-out or needy behavior persists.

We can't teach children to behave better by making them feel worse.

Punishing children for expressing their unmet emotional needs through their behavior makes children, who are already feeling disconnected, feel worse. Children behave better when they feel better. When we learn to decode behavior, and meet, or at least acknowledge the need that the behavior is communicating, the child changes her behavior. If the behavior is being caused by an unmet need, once the need is met or acknowledged, the child stops acting out since there is no longer an unmet need to communicate.

We begin the process of decoding children's behavior by asking, "What is causing this behavior?" How we answer that question is influenced by our beliefs about children. In our culture, adults believe and assume many negatives about children.

 In your Parenting Journal:

Make a list of ten of the most negative words you have ever heard anyone say about children.

In the parenting workshop, we make this list as a group.

These are ten of the most common words that appear on the list:

Rude – selfish – manipulative – brat – mean – disrespectful – noisy – messy – stupid – ungrateful

Whether or not we think we have any of these beliefs about children, if we heard those words often enough for them to appear on the list, they influence our thinking about children's behavior.

When we ask the question,"What is causing this behavior?" none of those beliefs about children can be the answer because those beliefs are judgments, not causes.

There are many causes for children's behavior. Some of the many causes of challenging behaviors are:

- unmet need for human connection

- unmet physical and/or emotional needs

- stress caused by a child's emotional environment

- environmental conditions that compromise a child's physical wellbeing

- physical and/or emotional sensitivities with which a child is born

- sensitivities that are part of a child's innate temperament

- physical and/or emotional sensitivities or challenges caused by stresses during and following birth

- sensory processing challenges

Behaviors are either caused or learned. Children imitate everything we say and do. Some of children's challenging behaviors are learned behaviors. We cannot expect children not to imitate behaviors that we model.

In your Parenting Journal:

Look at your list of button pushing behaviors and check mark any behaviors on your list that you model to learn if you are reinforcing unacceptable behaviors by modeling them.

While there are many causes for behavior, there are only four kinds of behavior.

Needy behavior – caused by an unmet physical or emotional need

Healing behavior – the release of emotional pain

Sensitivity or temperament behavior – reactions caused by innate temperament or physical or emotional sensitivities

Happy behavior – the state of well being when physical and emotional needs are met

Think about how children behave when they are happy. What do they do?

In your Parenting Journal:

Make a list of ten ways your children behave when they are happy.

In the parenting workshop, we make this list as a group. These are the ten most often cited happy behaviors:

Smiling – laughing – singing – humming – listening – sharing – helping – cooperating – hugging – playing

In your Parenting Journal or below:

Compare the "needy," button-pushing behaviors list to the happy behaviors list.

Needy behaviors:

Temper tantrums– whining – not listening – hitting – talking back – not cooperating – teasing – bullying – refusing to share –fighting with siblings – refusing to get dressed – refusing to brush teeth – arguing – calling names – hurting others

Happy behaviors:

Smiling – laughing – singing – humming – listening – sharing – helping – cooperating – hugging – playing

What do you notice about the two lists?

The behaviors listed are the opposite of each other. Children are happy when their needs are met and they are not in pain. They are not acting out because they have no hurts or unmet needs to communicate. Look back at your list of "needy," button-pushing behaviors and rename those behaviors as unhappy behaviors. Do you feel compassion or empathy for the child who is unhappy because he is in emotional pain or frustrated by an unmet need? Do you feel a shift in your attitude toward the child's behavior?

This shift in attitude about children's behavior is key to connection parenting, to parenting through love instead of fear.

A change of heart is the essence of all other change and is brought about by a re-education of the mind.
- Emmiline Pettrick Lawerence

When we get new information, our awareness changes.

New information: Children's acting-out behavior is the release of emotional pain, a communication of unmet need, or a sensitivity reaction.

When our awareness changes, our attitude changes.

New attitude: Now that I know this behavior is not a challenge to my authority, I want to find out what is hurting my child or what he needs.

When our attitude changes, our actions change.

New actions: You connect with the child by listening and letting him know you are on his side.

It is only when our actions change, that the outcome is different.

New outcome: When parents and children feel connected, they care about each other's needs and feelings, and they work together.

Meeting Children's Needs vs. Making Children Happy

When parents first hear about solving behavior problems through meeting children's needs, they often confuse meeting children's needs with making them happy.

What's the difference between meeting children's needs and making them happy?

Meeting children's needs does not always make them happy. Children **need** to brush their teeth to have oral health. Being told that it's time to brush their teeth may not make them happy. Telling children they can skip brushing their teeth would make them happy, but it wouldn't meet their "real" need to have a parent who will support them in having oral health.

Making children happy is different than trying to keep them from being unhappy.

If we bring home a puppy, we make children happy. Buying them a toy so that they won't cry when we say no is trying to keep them from being unhappy.

We often try to keep a child from being unhappy to meet our need for harmony. We know that if we pacify them, we won't have to listen to the release of feelings that the disappointment of not getting what they ask for may trigger.

When children ask for excessive material "things," it is because they have learned to try to fill their love cup with "things". It doesn't work for them any better than it works for us. We live in one of the most affluent societies in the world, yet our country has some of the most emotionally needy children in the world.

> ## Meeting children's emotional needs sometimes means loving them enough to say no and set limits.

Children push the limits when they need to release stored pain. They are pushing "for" a limit, not against it. Children push the limits by asking for candy, toys, or privileges to distract themselves from their pain. When we set the limit or say no, the no or the limit is the disappointment that overflows the hurts cup and allows children to release the pain that is making them unhappy.

Meeting children's emotional needs by saying no or setting a limit and then accepting and listening to their feelings, meets their "real" need, which is to release their painful feelings. Unless we learn to decode children's behavior, we won't know what the "real" need is.

> ## The discipline of decoding behavior is a five-step process.

The five steps are:

1. Disciplining yourself to resist reacting to the behavior

2. Remembering that behavior is a communication of need

3. Asking yourself the question, "What is causing this behavior-what is the intention behind the action?"

> i. Is this a physical or an emotional unmet need?
>
> ii. Is this the release of emotional pain?
>
> iii. Is this a sensitivity or temperament reaction?

4. Connecting by acknowledging that the child is expressing a need or a hurt.

5. Addressing the need or listening to the release of hurt.

Remember: Connect before you correct. Our brains only work well when we feel safe. To teach children acceptable ways to communicate their needs requires that they know we are on their side.

> *Children do well if they can, if they can't, we need to figure out why so we can help.*
> - *Ross W. Greene, Ph.D. author,* ***The Explosive Child***

Decoding unmet physical needs

When we ask, "What's causing this behavior?" It is easier to begin with unmet physical needs.

Examples:

"Is this child hungry, ill, or tired?"

"Is this child reacting to sensory overload?"

"Is this child reacting to stress overload?"

If there is no apparent physical cause for the behavior, we look for unmet emotional needs. To do so requires awareness of children's emotional needs.

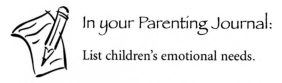 In your Parenting Journal:

List children's emotional needs.

In the parenting workshop, the group creates this list together. These are 25 of the most often identified emotional needs:

Unconditional love – loving touch – affection – acceptance – appreciation – attention – connection – respect – being listened to – guidance – safety – security – stability – down time – play – healthy self-esteem and self-worth – a sense of belonging – feeling valued – friendship – emotional release of pain – freedom – some control over their life – predictability – trust – positive role models.

Reviewing this list, do you think most children get these emotional needs met every day? Why do many children have unmet emotional needs?

Some of the reasons children have unmet emotional needs are:

• We lack information about children's emotional needs.

• We follow advice that goes against meeting our children's emotional needs.

• We can't pay attention to our children's needs because our attention is on *our* unmet needs.

• Children are not getting enough connection time.

Most often, the reason children have unmet emotional needs is that our lives are too busy and we don't have enough time to be with and connect with them. Parents' lives are too busy because there are not enough adult resources to do all that needs to be done. The loss of the extended family has been devastating to parenting and to childhood. Until there are more people to meet children's emotional needs, there will be unmet need behaviors to decode.

Decoding unmet emotional need behavior

One of the first signs that a child is feeling disconnected is a drop in the level of cooperation. When a child is uncooperative, we can take him gently aside and quietly ask, "What is this behavior about? What do you need?"

Even if the child cannot tell us, if the behavior is caused by an unmet emotional need, asking the question, "What do you need?" creates connection. The first step to cooperation is connection.

Remember:

The level of cooperation parents get from their children is usually equal to the level of connection children feel with their parents.

Decoding release of emotional hurt behaviors

When children's behaviors are physically or verbally hurtful to others, they need our help to find acceptable ways of releasing their emotional pain. We acknowledge the child's pain and provide the child with an acceptable outlet for releasing the pain. We say, "Stop hitting. I understand that you are hurting too, but you may not hit your brother. You may hit the "mad" pillow.

Decoding sensitivity reaction behaviors

If your child's emotional needs are fulfilled and the child's behavior still exhausts and frustrates you daily, your child may have sensitivity challenges. When we don't know that children's behaviors are reactions caused by their innate temperament or other sensitivities, we cannot support them in doing well. Children with sensitive temperaments or physical and emotional sensitivities and challenges want to do well, but they need additional support.

The following are some resources for parents who need information about other causes of challenging behaviors:

Raising Your Spirited Child by Mary Sheedy Kurcinka

The Explosive Child—New Approach for Understanding and Parenting Easily Frustrated and "Chronically Inflexible" Children, by Ross W. Greene Ph.D.

The Out-of-Sync Child by Carol Stock Kranowitz, Larry B. Silver

Smart Moves—Why Learning is Not All in Your Head, by Carla Hannaford Ph.D.

I am the Child, Using Brain Gym with Children with Special Needs, by Cecilia Freeman with Gail Dennison

Stopping Hyperactivity—Unique and Proven Program of Crawling Exercises for Overcoming Hyperactivity, by Nancy O'Dell and Patricia Cook

When we seek out information and resources, we find tools and support to help us, help our children, to do well.

It takes time to reprogram our reactions to children's acting out behaviors, to learn to decode behavior, and to learn about and teach restitution. While we are living in the gap between how we want to parent and developing our connection parenting skills, it is easier to stop using spanking and punishment if we have some loving alternatives in discipline.

It Wouldn't Hurt To Try the Following:

- When a small child is about to touch something dangerous or breakable, catch their hand, name the danger emphatically, "Hot!", then show them what they can touch instead.

- When children are about to do something dangerous, like going into the road or climbing on a bookcase, gather them into your arms, tell them "Danger!", and explain to them why their behavior frightens you. The word danger is more effective than saying "NO!".

- When you tell children to stop doing something ten times, you teach them they can do something ten times before you act. Speak once, and then go over and tell them what they can do instead. Telling children what we don't want them to do doesn't teach them what we do want them to do.

- Children need to be taught how to behave in stores, restaurants, etc. We can teach them at home by "playing" store or restaurant.

- Children need to be noticed and encouraged. When we give enough positive attention and connection, children don't have unmet emotional needs to communicate through acting out behavior.

- When a child is having a temper tantrum, the child is pouring out built-up hurts, disappointments, and frustrations. All we need to do is prevent children from hurting themselves, or anyone else and let them pour out their feelings. As soon as the feelings are released, their behavior improves.

• When you are stressed and feel yourself about to hit, announce loudly, "I'm feeling angry. I need this behavior to stop. I'm taking a time-out."

• For older children, make up a family code word or gesture to use in public that signals them to stop what they are doing.

Children who are "acting out" are usually trying to tell us, "I need more love."

The discipline of decoding behavior puts *discipline* into a new context. Discipline ceases to be the job of punishing children for their needy behaviors and becomes the job of meeting children's needs and teaching them self-discipline. Children's "acting–out" behaviors feel like a challenge to our parental authority. Our self-discipline is required to resist reacting to children's challenging behaviors. When we exercise self-discipline by choosing to decode behavior instead of punishing behavior, we teach children self-discipline by our modeling.

While learning to decode behavior may seem challenging, it makes the job of parenting more joyful and less a struggle. When we see parenting as the job of trying to control children's behavior, parenting is a struggle because *we cannot control children's behavior.* When we see our job as that of meeting children's needs, we enjoy our children, because *we can meet children's needs.*

Reconnecting with Teens

Ideally, we would begin building a strong connection with children before they are born, and nurture infants and children in the ways that protect, foster, and maintain that connection throughout infancy and childhood. However, if you didn't have the information or support to practice the nurturing that builds strong connections until now, you may have a teen who is struggling with issues of connection deficiency.

The younger children are when we increase connection, the more successful we will be at reconnection. Reconnecting with older children means we have to compensate. If teens are getting their connection needs met by their peers, then their peers have influence with them. Depending on the age and level of disconnection of your older child, you may need to do more than supplement your child's connection deficiency with more one-on-one connection time, to reestablish influence with your child.

If a connection deficiency, or physical or emotional sensitivities are causing extreme coping behaviors, teens and their parents need the support of professionals who specialize in healing therapies.

A resource for parents of children ages eleven through seventeen in crisis: KidsPeace National Centers for Kids in Crisis® www.kidspeace.org

The older children become, the more work it takes to establish or reestablish connection. It is never too late to strengthen your connection with your child. It is only late to do it easily.

Connection Parenting Is Proactive.

Children don't have a choice about being dependent on us to meet their emotional need for connection. We do have a choice about making it a priority to meet that need. Just as we plan to feed our children every day, we can plan to provide connection time every day.

There are three times in a day when children seem to need connection most. Unfortunately, they are the exact times when we feel we have the least to give. In the morning, we are hurrying to get out the door. When we first get home in the evening, we are hurrying to get dinner. At bedtime, we just want them to go to sleep so we can get a minute to ourselves for the first time all day. The needy behaviors that erupt at those times of the day are usually the result of children's emotional needs conflicting with our agenda.

Remember: It takes the same amount of time, attention, and energy to meet a child's emotional needs as it does to deal with the behaviors caused by unmet emotional needs. Either way, we spend the time. We become proactive parents, instead of reactive parents, when we make providing the connection children need, when they need it, part of our agenda.

Some examples of proactive parenting:

- Including five or ten minutes of one-on-one connection time in the morning can reduce morning conflicts and increase connection and cooperation

- Spending the first ten to twenty minutes upon arriving home, playing and being together can transform a needy, whiny, angry child into a happy child who wants to help us fix dinner

- Moving to an earlier "getting ready for bed" time allows us to connect before we are too tired. If we want sleep time to be 8 o'clock, then we plan bedtime for 7:30, so we have lots of time together before we say goodnight

It is as difficult for children to fall asleep when they are emotionally hungry as it is to fall asleep when they are physically hungry. The biggest reason children resist going to bed is that this is their last chance of the day for connection. It's also our last chance of the day to get our needs met. When we end up competing for those few evening hours, no one gets their needs met.

Since part-time parenting is going to continue until we make major changes in public policy toward valuing parenting, we need to do all we can to be proactive in meeting our children's emotional needs in our current circumstances. The more time we must spend away from our children trying to earn enough money to meet their physical needs, the more imperative it is to spend the precious time we do have, meeting everyone's emotional needs for connection.

*There is no single factor more radical in its
potential for healing the world than
a transformation in how we raise children.*
- Marianne Williamson

To move from coercion parenting to connection parenting, we need inspiration, information, resources, and support.

It is my honor, privilege, and joy to be one of the founding board members of an organization that provides all of these: the Alliance for Transforming the Lives of Children. www.atlc.org

The Alliance for Transforming the Lives of Children (aTLC)

Inspiration:

The Alliance for Transforming the Lives of Children is a consensus-based, interdisciplinary, not-for-profit organization of healthcare professionals, caregivers, scientists, educators, artists, parents, and children who share a deep and passionate concern for how we conceive, carry, birth, bond with, and care for children.

We know that caring for our children as whole, conscious beings has a profound impact on the adults they become; our intuition tells us this and modern science confirms it.

aTLC envisions a world where:

- Every child is wanted, welcomed, and valued.

- Every family is prepared and supported in the art and science of nurturing children.

- Adults honor childhood and respect each child's whole being.

- Children joyfully participate in the vital life of family and community.

aTLC is committed to:

- identifying the biological imperatives for developing our children as whole beings—physically, emotionally, and spiritually,

- defining the principles and specific actions that arise from these imperatives,

- making this information accessible to parents, caregivers, and policy makers,

- supporting families in implementing best parenting practices, and

- enhancing birthing and parenting practices throughout the world.

Information:

aTLC is assembling the most extensive collection of evidence – based research and information on the optimal nurturing of children ever assembled to be disseminated to parents.

A growing body of evidence now documents that the quality of people's childhood has a major impact on their entire life. This information is crucial to us all, at a time when families are facing the unprecedented pace and intensity of our high tech/low touch society. Neither medication nor the criminal "justice" system, address the root causes of the rapidly escalating rate of mental health disorders, addictions, violence, crime, and suicide evident among our young. At the core of this crisis is our culture's lack of awareness of the vital importance of a strong and healthy parent-child bond.

We believe, and research confirms, it is not enough for our society to diagnose and treat problems. We must prevent them. The Alliance is dedicated to promoting this essential parent-child connection that all children need to thrive.

In order to protect the wellbeing of our children and enrich the future of our society, aTLC is dedicated to supporting parents and professionals in making informed choices about consciously conceiving, birthing, and nurturing children. We gather and disseminate wisdom from many diverse sources, recommend standards, inspire research, and publicize current scientific evidence.

At the heart of aTLC are our *Proclamation* and evidence-linked *Blueprint for Transforming the Lives of Children.* These documents are a synthesis of leading scientific research and a distillation of ancient wisdom into specific Principles and Actions that will promote children's optimal growth and development.

Resources:

A core function of the Alliance is to link and support diverse organizations and individuals promoting innovative and progressive educational programs, services, products, and public policies that will transform the lives of children.

aTLC's website offers information and resources, and promotes dialog on conceiving, birthing, and parenting. The website includes aTLC's:

- Proclamation and Blueprint.
- A growing list of affiliated organizations and individuals who promote one or more aspects of the Blueprint.
- Recommended books, articles, and other resources.

Support:

The aTLC WarmLine: A Family Support Network

aTLC offers a phone-mentoring program to provide parents, parents-to-be, and caregivers support in applying the *aTLC Blueprint* of optimal parenting practices to everyday parenting concerns via a call-in center, ongoing parent mentoring sessions, and teleclasses.

Mentoring sessions are based on the following aTLC premises:

- A healthy parent/child bond, from preconception onward, is essential for effective parenting and a child's optimal physical, emotional, and spiritual development.

- Parents are doing the best they can, at any given moment, with the information, resources, and support they have.

- Children are doing the best they can—at any given moment—and their challenging behaviors are a way of communicating their need for adult attention, connection, and support.

- Children need a strong connection with their parents; it is never too late for parents to strengthen this connection with their children.

For information on accessing the aTLC Parent Support Network visit: www.aTLCWarmLine.org or call 1-800-460-6105

Other resources that have made a profound difference in my work with families are:

The Theraplay® Institute –
What is Theraplay®?

Theraplay is a short-term, therapist-guided play therapy for children and their parent/caregivers which:

- Enhances attachment, self-esteem and trust in others through joyful engagement

- Is based on the natural patterns of healthy interaction between parent and child

- Focuses on four essential qualities found in parent-child relationships: Structure, Nurture, Engagement, and Challenge

- Creates an active and empathic connection between child and parents

- Results in a changed view of the self as worthy and lovable, and of relationships as positive and rewarding

For information: www.theraplay.org

Or call 847-256-7334 in Wilmette, IL

Diane Gossen on Restitution-www.realrestitution.com
Offers books, videos, audiotapes, and training on teaching restitution in schools and in the family.

Chelsom Consultants Limited 134 110th Street,

Saskatoon, Sk S7N1S2

Call 1-800-450-4352 or email restitution@sasktel.net

Center for Non-Violent Communication^SM – A
global organization helping people connect with themselves and one another through Nonviolent Communication(sm), a process created by Marshall Rosenberg, Ph.D. www.cnvc.org

Brain Gym®
Educational Kinesiology is a program of physical activities that help children and adults build the neurological connections necessary for information to flow freely between the different parts of the brain and the body. Brain Gym activities help anyone who struggles with reading, writing, hyperactivity, following instructions, concentrating, remembering things, stress, anxiety, addiction, depression, confusing left and right,

maintaining hand/eye coordination, and being accident prone. Brain Gym activities assist those challenged with dyslexia, ADD, ADHD, and fetal alcohol syndrome.

Brain Gym is not only for those people with overt learning difficulties. All of us can benefit from Brain Gym activities. Olympic athletes use Brain Gym activities to reduce stress and improve performance. Brain Gym movements are simple and can be done at home, in school, at work, and in play.

For parents seeking a resource to help their children, Brain Gym is a win-win-win. The children get the tools and support they need to get their body/brain connections working better, the parents get these same benefits from doing the activities and movements with their children, and the parent/child relationship is strengthened by the time spent together doing the activities.

For information: www.braingym.org
Phone: (800) 356-2109 or (805) 658-7942

Brain Gym® International
1575 Spinnaker Drive, Suite 204B
Ventura, CA 93001

Academy for Coaching Parents International™

The Academy for Coaching Parents offers: training in coaching parents and families, marketing your business and positioning yourself as an expert in your community, and certifies your experience and education when requirements are met. Training in the early nurturing and bonding of the whole child—physical, emotional, social, mental, and spiritual—provides the connections spoken of in this book. Pam Leo is an Academy Instructor and teaches and certifies parent mentors in Connection Parenting.

Founder: Caron B. Goode, Ed.D.

Telephone: 520-979-4470

Web site: www.AcademyforCoachingParents.com or www.acpi.biz

The Institute of HeartMath® -

The Institute of HeartMath offers learning programs for improving student relations and academic performance, and helps adults transform stress, anxiety, and anger.

For information:

www.heartmath.org

Or call 831-338-8500 in Boulder Creek, CA

Touch the Future- A Nonprofit Learning Design Center

Inspired Resources for Parents, Educators, Caregivers & Coaches
www.ttfuture.org

In your Parenting Journal:

Practice decoding behaviors and meeting emotional needs. Look at your list of button-pushing behaviors and see how many problem behaviors you can solve by decoding the behavior and meeting the real need.

 It's All About WE: Rethinking Discipline Using Restitution by Diane Gossen, www.realrestitution.com

 Unconditional Parenting -Moving From Reward and Punishments to Love and Reason by Alfie Kohn

 Control Theory – A New Explanation of How We Control Our Lives by William Glasser, M.D.

 Time-Out... For Parents: A Compassionate Approach to Parenting by Cheri Huber & Melinda Guyol, MFCC

Chapter 7
Connecting through Meeting Our Own Needs

Families work best when everyone's needs are met.

For six chapters, we have focused on meeting children's needs. We have learned about children's emotional need for a strong connection and meeting that need by:

• Connecting and reconnecting with rewind, repair, and replay

• Treating children with respect

• Listening to children's needs and feelings

• Filling children's love cups

• Communicating in ways that build and maintain connection

• Decoding children's needy behaviors and responding to their needs instead of reacting to their behaviors

You now have six pieces of the parenting puzzle. The seventh and final piece of *Connection Parenting* is the "glue" that holds the puzzle together. That glue is meeting the needs of parents.

When flight attendants demonstrate the oxygen equipment on a plane, they instruct passengers, "If you are traveling with a young child, put on your own oxygen mask first, then assist the child."

Those same instructions apply to Connection Parenting. How well we parent depends, as much on how well we meet our needs, as it does on how well we meet children's needs.

We fill our children's cup best when our cup is full

Imagine the following scenario.

Your good friend gives you the gift of a day off from parenting. Your friend arrives at your home at 9 AM and says, "I'm giving you the day off. I'm taking over all your duties. The children will be cared for well. Here is some spending money, now go have a great day, and don't return until 5 o'clock."

You have time, childcare, and money and, because your children love this person and are excited about the day, you don't feel guilty about leaving them. You spend the whole day doing what you love to do. When you return at 5 o'clock, how do you feel about being with your children?

"My cup is filled and overflowing. I'm happy to see you. I have something to give, and I want to give it to you."

Children know how we feel about being with them. When we want to be with them they feel worthy of love and attention, and they believe they are loveable because we are attending to them with love and respect.

You cannot fill a child's cup if your cup is empty.

Our needs are as important as our children's needs. If our emotional needs were not met as children, we learned to believe that our needs were not important. We often try to meet those unmet needs by giving to others what we didn't get.

Contrast the first scenario with this one.

Your partner has been away on business all week. All three children have been sick. The car broke down. You had to call the plumber. The dog had to go to the vet. It's finally Friday afternoon and you are expecting a call telling you what time your partner will arrive. Instead, you get a call that the flight has been grounded due to fog and your partner can't get home until tomorrow. How do you feel about being with your children?

"My cup is empty and I have nothing more to give."

Children always know what we are feeling, but they don't always know why. When we don't want to be with children, they take it personally. They feel they must be unworthy of our love and attention. They believe they are unlovable instead of knowing that we have nothing left to give.

Connection Parenting is not child-centered parenting. Meeting the needs of children does not mean focusing so much on meeting their needs that we have no time or energy left for ours. No matter how much we know about meeting the emotional needs of children, we can only "do" what we know when our needs are met.

Parents' unmet needs create a cycle of stress

Have you ever wondered, "Why do my children have to be so needy and out of control when I am already so stressed?" We are not at our best when we are stressed and neither are children at their best when we are stressed.

Taking no time to meet our needs starts a vicious cycle. When our needs are not met, we become stressed. More stress means less connection with our children. The less we connect, the more children communicate their need for connection through acting-out behavior. The more children act out their needs, the more stressed we become.

Stress is contagious. We do get stress *from* our children but we also give it *to* them. It is difficult for children to feel content and be relaxed when they are with adults who are not feeling content and relaxed.

We parent better when our needs are met.

We don't do our best parenting when we are hurrying, worrying, overwhelmed, and stressed. When I ask parents when they feel best about their parenting, they recall vacation times, weekend times, or times when they have returned home from doing something relaxing. Imagine how different our parenting might be if we could meditate, do yoga, work out at the gym, get a massage, or do something we find relaxing every day. When parents have time for themselves they have more energy and attention for connecting with the children.

We are naturally more patient, understanding, and loving when we are relaxed.

We have four brainwave states. When we are relaxed, we are in either the alpha or theta brainwave state. Alpha is the relaxed state we would likely be in while meditating, walking in nature, knitting, painting a picture, playing a musical instrument, listening to soothing music, or gazing at an open fire. Theta is an even deeper state of relaxation where we access intuition, inspiration, and creativity. We are naturally more patient, understanding, and loving when we are relaxed.

When we are in deep sleep, we are in delta. When we are awake, alert, thinking, and active, we are in beta. Beta without alpha and theta is associated with stress, anxiety, and high blood pressure. If we spend too many of our days going from delta to beta, and back to delta without spending time in the relaxing brainwave states of alpha and theta we become stressed. We function better, and are healthier, when we spend some time each day in each of the four brainwave states.

I can only bring peace to my children when
I possess it myself.
- Katrina Kenison, author of **Mitten Strings for God**

We are more open to connection when relaxed.

Just as our stress affects children's behavior, our relaxation affects their behavior. I was telling a friend about children being able to connect more when parents are relaxed and she said, "That explains something to me. Whenever I sit down to knit, my daughter comes and sits near me and we have great conversations." Her revelation made me remember that when I did family day care, the days the children napped best were when I turned on a Mozart tape and knit while they napped. Children are more relaxed when the adults around them are relaxed.

Meeting the Needs of Parents

We need at least ten minutes a day alone to relax and connect with ourself. We need time to "just be" as much as our children do. Many busy parents go days without taking that time. When you make a commitment to have ten minutes a day to connect with yourself, you find ways to do it.

Some examples:

- Keeping a book in the car and allowing ten extra minutes to get where you are going will give you time to sit and read for ten minutes

- Taking a long bath instead of a quick shower on occasion

- Getting up ten minutes earlier to have a morning ritual of meditation, yoga, or reading the paper alone

- Creating a daily ten-minute workout

What you do for your ten minutes isn't as important as the benefit derived from the feeling of nurturing yourself.

Couples need to stay connected.

We need at least ten minutes a day to connect with our partners. When couples make a commitment to spend ten minutes a day connecting and get creative, they make it happen.

Some examples:
- Making a daily phone date to talk about anything but children, finances, and life maintenance
- Emailing love notes to each other daily
- Creating a ritual of giving each other a back, foot, hand, or head-massage daily

Taking ten minutes a day to stay connected is an investment in your relationship and in your children's security.

Single parents need to talk to another adult.

Single parents need at least ten minutes a day to connect with an adult family member or close friend. When single parents recognize and honor that need, they find ways to meet that need.

Some examples:

- Connecting with another single parent and using your daily "coffee break" to take turns listening to each other
- Connecting with another single parent and having a phone date each day to take turns listening to each other
- On days when all else fails, writing your thoughts and feelings in a journal gives you an outlet for feelings

When parents have someone to listen to their needs and feeling, they feel less isolated.

Parents Need Nurturing Too

If you are like most parents, you are so busy meeting your children's needs that you don't take time to nurture yourself.

Parents need a nurture-myself date every week.

Ten minutes a day is a great way to maintain feeling connected to yourself, but, at least once a week we need at least an hour to do something nurturing that fills our cup.

Couples need a date every week with their partner to nurture their relationship.

The lament I most hear from parents is "Since we had children, I never get to be alone with my partner." Many parents try to meet everyone's needs by "tag-team" parenting – working opposite hours so one of them can always be home with the children. No matter what working and parenting schedule parents have, couples need time alone together to connect and fill each other's cup.

Single parents need a nurturing date every week with a friend or family member.

Single parents have to keep filling their children's love cups every day without any one there to fill their cup. Single parents need nurturing from others.

Keeping your Love Cup Full

Take five minutes now to think about what nurtures you. Remember how you nurtured yourself before you had children.

 ## In your Parenting Journal:

List at least ten activities that you find nurturing.

Sample "Nurturing Myself" List:

Taking a walk on the beach

Working out at the gym

Having a date with my partner

Taking a nap

Reading a book

Playing or listening to music

Going for a hike

Meditating

Taking a bubble bath

Playing my favorite sport

In your Parenting Journal:

Check-mark the activities on your "Nurturing Myself" list that you do on a regular basis. How many do you do?

The number of nurturing activities you check-marked on your "Nurture Myself" list shows how you unconsciously rate the importance your needs.

0 – My needs don't matter at all.

1 – 2 My needs matter but not as much as my children's needs

3 – 6 My needs are important

7 – 10 My needs matter as much as my children's needs

In your Parenting Journal:

List your reasons for not doing what is on your "Nurturing Myself" list.

In my classes, the reasons parents cite most often are time, energy, childcare, guilt, and money.

Time: I don't have enough time to do all the things I have to do, spend time with my children, and still have time for my needs.

Energy: By the time I get the kids in bed at night, I don't have any energy left to do something for myself.

Childcare: I don't have anyone to care for my children so I can do something for myself.

Guilt: When I do get some free time, I feel too guilty to use that time for myself, instead of spending it with the family.

Money: I can't afford to pay for childcare so I can do something for myself. Some of the things I want to do cost money. I cannot afford the extra money to pay for the activity that would fill my cup.

None of us can do parenting well alone.

Lack of resources and support prevent us from doing what we need to do to nurture ourselves. Unless parents have a lot of support, they rarely take time for themselves or spend time alone with their partner. Few families today have the support of a live-in grandparent, aunt, uncle, or a nanny. Whether your family consists of a single parent and one child; a mom, a dad, and three children; two partners and two children, or a blended family with multiple moms, dads, and step-siblings, families need more resources and support.

The key to Connection Parenting is more resource.

Without the support of others to share in caring for the children, it is impossible to meet everyone's needs. Creating more resources makes it possible for parents to get their needs met. Children need to know, trust, and depend on people other than their parents. A "tribe" is the missing element that families need to thrive.

We re-create the "tribe" by creating an "extended family of choice." We adopt people we love and care about to be "honorary" aunts, uncles, and grandparents.

Creating Resource

For those without the support of a biological extended family, we create "extended family of choice" by inviting elderly neighbors, single-parent families, and non-parent friends and co-workers to come to dinner and do things with our family. These gatherings cultivate relationships that benefit the parents, the children, and the friends. The more children get to know and love other adults, the more people they have to give them love, attention, and connection. When children have connections with other adults, parents don't have to meet all their emotional needs.

For those parents with very young children, it is usually easier to be away during the day than at bedtime. One way for parents to have more time alone together is to have mini-dates at non-traditional date times. Rather than trying to find a babysitter so they can go to dinner and a movie on a Saturday night, parents often find more childcare options if they go out for a Saturday or Sunday morning brunch.

For those with older children, it works well to alternate childcare with another family. All the children spend the evening at one family's house while the other parents get to have a date or time for themselves. The next time they switch. The children love it, it doesn't cost money, and the parents get a break and an opportunity to connect regularly.

For adults who parent alone for many hours, whether it's because of being a single parent or because the other parent is working, hiring a young person, between the ages of ten and fourteen, as a parent helper can make a big difference. Paying an older child a few dollars an hour to come in after school, to play with the children for an hour or two gives a parent the resource to take a little break, make dinner, make phone calls, or spend one-on-one time with one of the children.

For single parents, connecting with other single parents can provide nurturing to fill your cup. Connect with another single parent and do weekly dinner swaps. One day a week, each parent makes double of a meal and gives the other parent a night off from making dinner. Better yet, take turns having each other over for dinner once a week.

Getting together, to help each other work, is a fun way to create more resource for everyone. The adults rotate being with the children, while the other adults help each other get dinner, or get some projects done around the house or the yard. The adults aren't isolated, the children have fun, and the work is done.

When there are more people to care for the children, everyone gets more of their needs met.

I have found some answers to creating resource, but there are more answers to be found when we get inspired to be creative about how we can work together to meet everyone's needs.

Let us put our minds together and see what kind of life we can make for our children. - *Chief Sitting Bull*

Nurturing children is not only the job of parents. We all have a stake in how well children's connection needs are met. The children of today will be our world leaders before we know it. I want to live in a world with adults whose childhood emotional needs were met.

Practicing Creating Resource

 In your Parenting Journal:

Make a list of your existing support network.

Make a list of "possible" support people with whom you could cultivate a relationship to expand your tribe.

Make a list of creative ideas for doing more of the activities on your "Nurturing Myself List".

Make a list of the people you want to tell about Connection Parenting.

Epilogue

We want life to be better for our children than it was for us. Connection Parenting is win-win parenting. We make life better for children when we connect with others to create enough resource to meet everyone's needs.

Children not only depend on us to meet their needs and build a strong connection, they also depend on us to be a model of what it looks like to be a happy, loving, peaceful adult, whose life has joy, meaning, and purpose. The best gift we can give to our children is to become that model by parenting through love and connection.

This is the end of this book and what I hope will be the beginning of a worldwide advance in returning to the nurturing parenting that human beings need to thrive.

 *Mitten Strings for God* by Katrina Kenison

The following poem is dedicated to all parents who are striving to give the nurturing they didn't get.

Pam Leo

I Was Born To Love

I was born to love.
I was born lovable.
I was born carrying my seed of love.

I was born with needs.
Back then it was up to others to nurture my seed.
All I could do was need.
Because other's seeds had not been nurtured,
Their seeds of love had not blossomed
And they could not nurture my seed.

Without that nurturing, my seed could not sprout.
The love I was born with stayed locked inside.
Many years of unmet needs and unhealed wounds
Have buried my seed.
But that seed of love is still inside of me.

I was born to love.
It is my right and my responsibility
To do the digging that will uncover my seed of love.
I can heal my wounds
I can nurture my seed of love.
My seed of love can still sprout and grow.
I can blossom into the loving being
I was born to be.
But now, it is up to me.

- Pam Jo Leo

Acknowledgments

When I read the acknowledgments in books, the authors often say that their books could not have been written without the support of the people they acknowledge.

Now, having written my first book, I understand why they say that. It's true.

Since there is no way I can ever repay all of you who inspired me, taught me, believed in me, encouraged me, and supported me emotionally, financially, and technically, I now appreciate you publicly.

My loving thanks

- to Caron B. Goode, my editor, mentor, and angel, for your trust, patience, humor, heart, spirit, wisdom, skill, encouragement, and support

- to Nancy Cleary, my publisher and fairy goddess-mother, for your belief in this book from the first moment, your energy, your flexibility, your listening, leadership, patience, "smiles" and philanthropy of creativity

- to my mother, Eleanor Carver, for teaching me the meaning of steadfast love

- to Carmine, for keeping your promise to help me deliver my message to the world

- to Tate, for being "the kettle tender"

- to my brother, Brad, for supplying me with a computer and always fixing anything that needed fixing

- to my sister, Kathie, for your nurturing and caring

- to Grammie Jan and Grandad Merton, for all the child care, meals, encouragement, cookies, and comfort

- to Leigh Baker, for all the years of your love, friendship, listening, and generosity

- to Henry, for keeping my old cars running all these years

- to my women's group of 18 years , Kathie, Debbie, Wendy, Vicki, and Cat, for being there for me through it all

- to Nancy, John and Leah, for all the childcare/play-dates that gave me time to write

- to the moms in my Parent Resource mother's group, for your endless support in endless ways

- to Joseph Chilton Pearce, for your information, inspiration, and model

- to the board members of the Alliance for Transforming the Lives of Children, for hearing my voice and welcoming me into the choir

- to Lisa Reagan, for recognizing the importance of Connection Parenting and insisting I needed to know Caron B. Goode

- to all the children, for teaching me about the needs of children

- to all the parents, for allowing me to learn from their struggles and successes

- to my first born daughter Leah B, for inspiring my quest for answers and for now joining me in the quest

- to my second born daughter, Sage, for loving me all the while I struggled to become a better parent, and for giving me three beautiful grandchilren

- to my grandchildren, Magnolia, Lily, and Fox for the joy you bring to my life and for teaching me there will always be more to learn about meeting the needs of children

- to Darline, my bosom friend, for thirty-seven years of devoted friendship, and for being the only person in the world who is as excited as I am that I have an ISBN number

- to Marilyn, for your eleventh hour support

- to Jack, my favorite PITA, for more than I can say

- to Wendy, at Parent & Family, for keeping me writing all these years

- to Jane Sheppard, for writing such an awesome foreword

- to all the authors who were my mentors, for their books that gave me the pieces of the puzzle

Recommended Books for Connection Parenting

"A parenting philosophy is relevant only to the extent that it promotes parenting practices which support secure bonding." - Pam Leo

These books promote birth and parenting practices that support strong parent-child bonds. Some books are appropriate for multiple categories and may be listed more than once.

Pregnancy, Birth & Bonding:

The Continuum Concept
by Jean Liedloff

**The Vital Touch: How Intimate Contact With
Your Baby Leads to Happier, Healthier Development**
by Sharon Heller, Ph.D.

**Untouched: The Need for Genuine Affection
in an Impersonal World**
by Mariana Caplan, M.A.

Touching: The Human Significance of the Skin
by Ashley Montagu

Infant Massage: A Handbook for Loving Parents
by Vimala Schneider McClure

From One Child to Two
by Judy Dunn

Welcoming Your Second Baby
by Vicki Lansky

The Baby Book
by William and Martha Sears

The Birth Book
by William and Martha Sears

The Pregnancy Book
by William and Martha Sears

Nighttime Parenting
by William Sears, Mary White

Mind Over Labor
by Carl Jones

The Birth Partner
by Penny Simkin

Attachment Parenting: Instinctive Care for Your Baby and Young Child
by Katie Allison Granju

The Family Bed
by Tine Thevenin

Magical Child
by Joseph Chilton Pearce

The Aware Baby: A New Approach To Parenting
by Aletha J. Solter, Ph.D.

Birth Without Violence
by Frederick LeBoyer

Parenting & Optimal Nurturing:

The Seven Habits of Highly Effective Families
by Steven R. Covey

Parent-Teen Breakthrough: The Relationship Approach
by Myra Kirshenbaum and Charles Foster

The Natural Child–Parenting from the Heart
by Jan Hunt

Your Child's Self Esteem
by Dorothy C. Briggs

The Vital Touch: How Intimate Contact With Your Baby Leads to Happier, Healthier Development
by Sharon Heller, Ph.D.

Untouched: The Need for Genuine Affection in an Impersonal World
by Mariana Caplan, M.A.

Touching: The Human Significance of the Skin
by Ashley Montagu

Infant Massage: A Handbook for Loving Parents
by Vimala Schneider McClure

Real Boys: Rescuing Our Sons from the Myths of Boyhood
by William Pollack and Mary Pipher

The Aware Baby: A New Approach To Parenting
by Aletha J. Solter, Ph.D.

Helping Young Children Flourish
by Aletha J. Solter, Ph.D.

When Your Kids Push Your Buttons
by Bonnie Harris

I Love You Rituals
by Becky A. Bailey, Ph.D.

Magical Child
by Joseph Chilton Pearce

Theraplay: Helping Parents and Children Build Better Relationships Through Attachment-Based Play
by Ann M. Jernberg Phyllis B. Booth

The Family Bed
by Tine Thevenin

Raising Resilient Children
by Robert Brooks, Ph.D. and Sam Goldstein, Ph.D.

Nighttime Parenting
by William Sears, Mary White

Beyond the Rainbow Bridge: Nurturing our children from birth to seven
by Barbara Patterson

The Irreducible Needs Of Children: What Every Child Must Have To Grow, Learn and Flourish
by T. Berry Brazelton, M.D. and Stanley I. Greenspan, M.D.

Listening To Children (series of 8 small booklets)
by Patty Wipfler
-- Crying
-- Healing Children's Fears
-- Setting Limits With Children
-- Tantrums and Indignation
-- Reaching For Your Angry Child
-- Supporting Adolescents
-- Playlistening
-- Special Time

Everyday Blessings: The Inner Work of Mindful Parenting
by Myla and John Kabot-Zinn

Siblings Without Rivalry
by Faber & Mazlish

Mitten Strings for God: Reflections for Mothers in a Hurry
by Katrina Kenison and Melanie Marder Parks

Unconditional Parenting–Moving from Rewards and Punishment to Love and Reason
by Alfie Kohn

Behavior & Discipline:

It's all about WE: Rethinking Discipline Using Restitution
by Diane Gossen

Easy To Love, Difficult To Discipline: The 7 Basic Skills for Turning Conflict into Cooperation
by Becky A. Bailey, Ph.D.

For Your Own Good: Hidden Cruelty in Child-Rearing and the Roots of Violence
by Alice Miller

High Risk: Children Without A Conscience
by Magid and McKelvey

Tears and Tantrums: What to Do When Babies and Children Cry
by Aletha J. Solter, Ph.D.

Building The Bonds of Attachment: Awakening Love In Deeply Troubled Children
by Daniel A. Hughes

Pam Leo

Theraplay: Helping Parents and Children Build Better Relationships Through Attachment-Based Play
by Ann M. Jernberg Phyllis B. Booth

Playful Parenting
by Lawrence J. Cohen, Ph.D.

Punished by Rewards: The Trouble with Gold Stars, Incentive Plans, A's, Praise, and Other Bribes
by Alfie Kohn

Raising Your Spirited Child
by Mary Sheedy Kurcinka

Kids, Parents and Power Struggles
by Mary Sheedy Kurcinka

Time-Out... For Parents: A Compassionate Approach to Parenting
by Cheri Huber & Melinda Guyol, MFCC

The Explosive Child: A New Approach for Understanding and Parenting Easily Frustrated, Chronically Inflexible Children
by Ross W. Greene

The Out-Of-Sync Child: Recognizing and Coping With Sensory Integration Dysfunction
by Carol Stock Kranowitz and Larry B. Silver

Education & Activities:

Miseducation: Preschoolers at Risk
by David Elkind

Learning All The Time
by John Holt

Escape From Childhood
by John Holt

Dumbing Us Down
by John Taylor Gatto

Seven Times the Sun: Guiding Your Child Through the Rhythms of the Day
by Shea Darian

The Children's Year: Crafts & Clothes for Children and Parents to Make
by Stephanie Cooper, Christine Fynes-Clinton and Marye Rowling

Earthways: Simple Environmental Activities for Young Children
by Carol Petrash, Donald Cook

Roots, Shoots, Buckets & Boots: Gardening Together With Children
by Sharon Lovejoy

Communication and Relationships:

Getting the Love You Want
by Harville Hendrix

How to Talk So Kids Will Listen and Listen So Kids Will Talk
by Faber & Mazlish

Nonviolent Communication: A Language of Life
by Marshall B. Rosenberg, Ph.D.

I Need Your Love: Is That True?
By Byron Katie

Getting Real
by Susan Campbell

Saying What's Real
by Susan Campbell

Personal Growth:

The Power of Now
by Eckhart Tolle

Loving What Is
by Byron Katie

The Power of Intention
by Wayne Dyer

Excuse Me, Your Life Is Waiting
by Lynn Grabhorn

Magazines and Periodicals:

byronchild – The magazine for progressive families – Australia

Mothering Magazine
Edited by Peggy O'Mara

Connecting! e-Newsletter from the Parents Leadership Institute
by Patty Wipfler

**Empathic Parenting The Journal of the Canadian Society
for the Prevention of Cruelty to Children**

Connection Parenting Links

"A parenting philosophy is relevant only to the extent that it promotes parenting practices which support secure bonding."

These sites promote birth and parenting practices that support strong parent-child bonds:

Birth

Academy of Certified Birth Educators http://www.acbe.com/

Association of Labor Assistants and Childbirth Educators http://www.alace.org/

Association of Nurse Advocates for Childbirth Solutions (ANACS) http://www.anacs.org/

Birthing from Within, An Extraordinary Approach To Childbirth http://www.birthpower.com/

Birth Roots http://ourbirthroots.org

Birthing the Future http://www.birthingthefuture.com/

Doulas of North America http://www.dona.com/

Gentle Birth Choices (Waterbirth) http://www.waterbirth.org/

Hypnobirthing Institute of New York http://www.hypnobirthingnyc.com/

Midwifery Today Magazine http://www.midwiferytoday.com/

Mother-Friendly Childbirth http://www.motherfriendly.org/

National Association of Childbearing Centers
http://www.BirthCenters.org/

Parenting

Academy for Coaching Parents http://www.acpi.biz/

Alfie Kohn (Author) http://www.alfiekohn.org/

Association for Pre- & Perinatal Psychology and Health
http://www.birthpsychology.com/apppah/

ATLC Warmline http://www.atlcwarmline.org/

Attachment Parenting International
http://www.attachmentparenting.org/

Aware Parenting Institute http://www.awareparenting.com/

Bonnie Harris (author) http://www.bonnieharris.com/

Canadian Society for the Prevention of Cruelty to Children
http://www.empathicparenting.org/

Compleat Mother Magazine,
http://www.compleatmother.com/

Families for Natural Living
http://www.familiesfornaturalliving.org/

Infant-Parent Institute http://www.infant-parent.com/

Inspired Parenting http://www.inspiredparenting.net/home/

Mother Magazine, The http://www.themothermagazine.co.uk/

Mothering Magazine http://www.mothering.com/

Myrna B. Shure Thinking Child
http://www.thinkingpreteen.com/

The Natural Child Project http://www.naturalchild.com/home/

Northwest Attachment Parenting http://www.nw-ap.org/

The Search Institute http://www.search-institute.org/

http://www.kidflourish.com/ Tom Adams Kids Flourish

Education

American Homeschool Association
http://www.americanhomeschoolassociation.org/

Waldorf Homeschoolers
http://www.waldorfhomeschoolers.com/

Discipline

Becky A. Bailey, Ph.D.   (Author of Easy to Love, Difficult to
Discipline) http://www.beckybailey.com/

Center for Effective Discipline http://www.stophitting.com/

Diane Gossen Restitution for Children
http://www.realrestitution.com/

Family Research Laboratory, University of New Hampshire
http://www.unh.edu/frl/index.html

Murray Strauss, Co-Director of the Family Research Laboratory http://pubpages.unh.edu/~mas2/

No Spanking Page, The http://www.neverhitachild.org/
Project NoSpank http://nospank.net/

Don't Shake Jake   (Prevent Shaken Baby Syndrome)
http://www.dontshakejake.org/

Optimal Nurturing

Alliance for Transforming the Lives of Children
http://www.atlc.org/

byronchild Magazine http://byronchild.com

Holistic Pediatric Association http://hpakids.org

La Leche League http://www.lalecheleague.org/

Mothering Magazine http://mothering.com

Liedloff Society for the Continuum Concept, The
http://www.continuum-concept.org/

Parents Leadership Institute, Patty Wipfler, Listening to Children
http://www.parentleaders.org/

Nurture by Nature Network http://www.nurturebynature.org/

Playful Parenting, Lawrence J. Cohen, Ph.D.
http://www.playfulparenting.com/

Raising Resilient Children
http://www.raisingresilientkids.com/

Rebozo Way Project, The http://www.rebozoway.org/

Theraplay Institute http://www.theraplay.org/

Touch the Future http://www.ttfuture.org/

Genital Integrity

Doctors Opposing Circumcision
http://faculty.washington.edu/gcd/DOC/

National Organization of Circumcision Information Resource
Centers http://www.nocirc.org/

Nurses for the Rights of the Child http://www.cirp.org/nrc/

The Ashley Montagu Resolution to End the Genital Mutilation
of Children Worldwide: A Petition to the World Court, the
Hague (Please visit this site and sign the petition.)
http://Montagunocircpetition.org/index.php?pcf=home

Personal Growth

Center for Nonviolent Communication, The
http://www.cnvc.org/

Getting Real Seminars and Coaching
http://www.susancampbell.com/

LifeCoaching.com http://www.lifecoaching.com/

Wellness Associates http://www.thewellspring.com/

World Cafe, The http://www.theworldcafe.com/

Index

A

abandonment, as threat, 25
Academy for Coaching
Parents International,
160–161
acceptance, need for, 61
acknowledgement, 82
acting-out, 28, 150
actions, 141
ADD, 159–160
addiction, 159–160
ADHD, 159–160
adolescents. *see* teens
advice, conflicting, 68–69
affection, demanding, 47–48,
51–52
Alliance for Transforming the
Lives of Children (aTLC),
154–158
anger, 67, 150
anxiety, 159–160
apologizing, 45, 47–48, 49
appreciation, 117–119
arguing, 124
attachment parenting, 18
aTLC. *see* Alliance for
Transforming the Lives of
Children (aTLC)
attention deficit/hyperactivity
disorder, 159–160
attention, need for, 60–61, 82
attitude, 141
authoritative parenting, 19
authority, uncooperative
behavior and, 23
awareness, 141

B

babies' cries, 126
back talk, 124
Bailey, Becky, 91
Baldwin, James, 44
bedtime, 153
behavior
    acting-out, 28, 150
    causes of, 138
    as a communication of
    need, 125–127
    control of, 150
    decoding, 128–129,
    143–144, 146–147
    describing, 115–116
    feelings and, 121
    happiness and, 139–140
    hurt, 147
    problems with. *see* behav-
    ior problems
    sensitivity reaction, 147
behavior problems
    button pushing and, 124
    control behaviors and, 62
    lack of cooperation, 23
    modeling and, 139
    needs of children and, 27
    self-esteem and, 28
    workshops and, 123
birth, 16, 78, 155
blaming, 108
Bombeck, Erma, 43–44
bonding
    adult, 87
    cooperation from children
    and, 54

L

language, 58, 99–100,
124–125, 137–138
laughing, 84–85
Lawerence, Emmiline
Pettrick, 141
learning difficulties, 159–160
learning styles, 39–40
lecturing, 108
Leidloff, Jean, 123
Leo, Pam Jo, 178
"let's", 53
lifestyles, modern, 121–123
limits, seeking, 65, 143
listening
    as button pushing behav-
    ior, 124
    to children's communica-
    tion, 126–127
    connecting through, 57, 74
    diminished ability to,
    71–72
    healing emotional hurts
    and, 66
    with love, 101–102
    meeting emotional needs
    by, 86
    practice with, 59–60
    speaking in a way to
    encourage, 100–104
love
    connection and, 86
    cup. see love cup
    hitting and, 130
    listening with, 101–102
    of self, 92
    teaching, 46
    unconditional, 79
love cup
    filling our children's, 97

filling our own, 164, 165
importance of filling daily,
87–88
materialism and, 143
one-on-one connection
time and, 85–86
play and, 82–85
as problem prevention, 87
rituals and, 91–92
time, high-quality and,
81–82

M

Magical Child, 41, 45
manipulating children,
116–117
manners, 45, 47–48, 49
materialism, 16, 142–143
media as form of separation
from family, 17
memory difficulties, 159–160
Michelangelo, 31
modeling
    apologizing and, 50
    coercion and, 48
    conflict resolution skills,
    24–25
    limitations of, 54
    manners and, 49
    parenting and, 27
    of respect, 44–46
    sharing and, 50–51
    as teaching tool, 134
modern lifestyles, 121–123
money, lack of, 173

N

name calling, 108, 124
nature, 95

needs of children
  acceptance, 61
  articulation of, 124–125
  attention, 60–61
  behavior and, 125–127
  behaviors and, 27
  connection, 77–79
  decoding, 144–145,
  146–147
  emotional, 146–147
  happiness versus, 142–143
  importance of meeting,
  17–18, 20
  versus needs of others,
  24–25, 28
  parents' job to meet, 51–52
  parents' presence, 27
  physical, 144–145
  punishment and, 135–137
  wants and, 125
  yelling and, 100
needs of parents
  adults' job to meet, 51–52
  connection to partner, 169
  importance of meeting,
  163–164
  not being met as children,
  165
  nurturing, 170–171
  parenting ability and,
  166–167
  relaxation, 167–168
  resources, 173–176
  stress and, 166
  time off of parenting, 164
  ways to meet, 168–169
needs, stating, 109, 110, 115
"no", 112–113, 143
Noelle, Scott, 30–31
Nolte, Dorothy Law, 41
nonverbal communication,
124–125, 150

Nonviolent Communication
(NVC) Process, 109–110, 128
noticing, 117–119, 149
nurture, 95

O

observation, 109, 110, 111
"ok", 115
one-on-one connection time,
85–86, 88–91, 153
orders, 52, 106–107
outdoing, 59

P

parenting
  advice, 68–69
  Alliance for Transforming
  the Lives of Children
  (aTLC) and, 154–158
  anger and, 69–70
  authoritative, 19
  challenges, 34, 34–35
  child-centered, 165–166
  by coercion, 19–21, 48, 54
  diminished ability to listen
  and, 71–72
  education, 29–32
  forgiveness of self and, 29
  goals, 32–33
  healing own emotional
  hurts, 72–73
  journal. see journaling
  modeling and, 24–25, 27,
  44–46
  single, 169–171, 175
  strengths, 34
  tools, 37–38
partner connection, 169
past, bringing up, 63, 71
Pearce, Joseph Chilton, 41,
45

W

Y

We empower mom writers.

Publishing the Works of Extraordinary Mom Writers

Wyatt-MacKenzie Publishing, Inc.
WyMacPublishing.com

Printed in the United States
206601BV00001B/190/A